LIVING IN
BUT NOT OF
THE WORLD

LIVING IN

BUT NOT OF

THE WORLD

SHARLENE

WELLS

HAWKES

DESERET BOOK COMPANY

SALT LAKE CITY, UTAH

Library of Congress Cataloging-in-Publication Data

Hawkes, Sharlene Wells, 1964–
   Living in but not of the world / by Sharlene Wells Hawkes.
    p.   cm.
   Includes index.
   ISBN 1-57345-203-3 (hb)
    1. Christian life—Mormon authors. 2. Hawkes, Sharlene Wells,
   1964–   . I. Title.
   BX8656.H38   1997
   248.4'893—dc21
                                                  97-25702
                                                    CIP

Printed in the United States of America   49510

10   9   8   7   6   5   4   3   2   1

To Mom and Dad,

who set the highest of standards—

not only by their words but most especially by their deeds—

and who nurtured in me the courage

to be bold in my beliefs before the world.

They taught me what I hope to teach my own children:

to always "stand for truth and righteousness"

and to "let [my] light so shine"!

CONTENTS

PREFACE

You probably noticed the stark black-and-white cover of this book. I chose those contrasting colors specifically as an illustration of everything I hope to convey here.

I have found that standards, beliefs, values, and even simple rules are much easier to live when the lines are clearly drawn. If we think of our governing ethics in black-and-white terms, then no gray areas can cloud our determination to stay the course. When we're undecided about how we stand, we're in the gray area, and we sometimes let others lead us to choose the wrong. Why give other people the right, even the privilege, of directing *your* life? Decide now to keep everything in black and white, and then living in the world doesn't have to be a fretful experience but, rather, an exhilarating adventure in which you know you can trust yourself . . . and God.

ACKNOWLEDGMENTS

I have to be completely honest: this book is all my dad's idea. He came up with the concept, assisted in the development of chapters, and prodded me along continuously for more than three years, asking me every time we spoke, "How's the book coming?" I would still be working on chapter one if not for his constant checkups. Come to think of it, this wouldn't be a book at all if not for Dad. There are two things in particular that I love about Dad: first, his enthusiastic, never-ending flow of ideas, and second, his love of adventure. These two traits make a powerful combination that should have put Dad on top of Mount Everest by now—but I suppose the last twenty years, filled with stake conferences, mission tours, meetings, and interviews as he has served the Lord full-time, have kept him just a little too busy for such trivial adventures as mountain climbing. His greatest adventures have been those of the Spirit. He'll have to write a book about that someday. I'll keep bugging him about it.

I could not have undertaken a project such as this without depending, in addition, on Mom. Once a week, the kids and I would go over to Grandma and Grandpa's house, and she would watch them all day while I worked on the computer. That's why it took three years. But Mom's help is the reason I could finish this book. And to see Mom taking over for me yet again so I could focus on a project reminded me of the countless times I brought home loads of laundry during my college years and she insisted (I promise, she did!) on doing the laundry so I could write a paper. Or she would spend hours and hours working on my Miss America dress so I could focus on my mental preparation. She seems to take great satisfaction and joy from being the support we all lean on right before heading out into the world. That's the kind of mom I want to be.

Thanks also are due to my love and best friend, Bob, who takes all my projects in stride and never discourages, only encourages me. His ideas and philosophies have had a tremendous impact on my own way of thinking. Every now and then I catch him looking a little amused at all the balls I attempt to juggle at once. As I bustle about, usually with our three little girls in tow, I am constantly grateful to the Lord for this man who is as solid as the mountains.

Thank you to my friends who have allowed me to share their stories; to Richard Peterson of Deseret Book for taking my manuscript with its rough edges and smoothing it into presentable (and publishable) form; to my good friend Sheri Dew of Deseret Book for her support and encouragement; to Linda Gundry of Deseret Book for her final review and excellent suggestions; and to the Church's Department of Public Affairs for their specific help in addressing commonly asked questions. An additional "thank you" to Dad, Mom, Bob, and my sister Elayne for reviewing the manuscript in search of discrepancies and mistakes.

And to the reader, I hope this book serves as a resource and encouragement to you as you go about living your standards in a mostly standard-free world. It might be a little tricky at times, but I promise, it doesn't have to be hard!

INTRODUCTION

T oday, many Latter-day Saints find themselves living far away from centers of LDS strength. Because of schooling or career opportunities, or simply because of family ties to a particular geographical location, many of us are not surrounded by others of our faith, and instead we live among and work with people who know little of our distinctive beliefs and practices. Yet, no matter where we live, all of us will no doubt at some time or another have to stand up for our religion and explain our "peculiar" behavior. Even those of us who do live in areas where LDS chapels can be found, perhaps within blocks of each other, have opportunities to speak up for our beliefs.

Minutes after I was crowned Miss America, I was the focus of hundreds of reporters and their nosy inquiries—and I quickly learned that my entire life had become an open book and that representatives of the media felt it was their duty to read and interpret every word. If I had not been sure of who I was, what I believed in, and what I stood for, I could not have calmly and assuredly responded to this invasion on my privacy. Imagine for a moment that you have been singled out from an auditorium of, say, a thousand people and then brought to the front, where a blinding spotlight and a sensitive microphone greet you. You are then left alone. The questions are shouted out: What things are important to you? What do you believe in? Describe the kind of person you are. What do you stand for? If those questions are easy for you to answer, you may feel comfortable sitting in the spotlight all day. If not, the temperature could rise pretty quickly.

Can Latter-day Saints live *in* the world without becoming corrupted *by* the world? Is it possible to live in "Babylon" without being weakened spiritually by what goes on there? Without compromising their standards, can members of the Church live, work, study, and raise their families in places where members of the Church are in the minority? Is it possible to remain faithful while associating and working with people who live mostly to "eat, drink, and be merry"?

Of course it is! There are countless examples of those who have succeeded in doing so. And not only do they maintain their focus on the gospel standards while in the workplace or in their communities, but they are also making a difference in the lives of those they meet by communicating exactly what they stand for and why it brings them peace. And they do it in quiet, simple ways.

John and Cathy Barclay have been members of the Church for some ten years. My husband, Bob, and I have known them for about nine of those years—ever since we first met as members of the same ward in Massachusetts. Cathy is a part-time hairstylist and John, a businessman. After their baptism, both of them took their new roles as members of the Church very seriously—and they taught us "old" members a thing or two! I was impressed by the loving and sincere conversations Cathy would have with her clients, often leading them into discussions about the Savior in their lives and the common love they shared for Him. People knew she was a Christian *and* a Mormon as she helped teach them about what we, as Mormons, stand for.

John works with two partners, both of whom belong to different churches. But as Christians, the three of them determined that they would give their mission statement at the beginning of each meeting with new clients. They explain that they are "God-fearing and Christian-centered men" whose creed is integrity, and then they proceed with the presentation. Says John: "We have had nothing but favorable response. Clients like knowing we have a belief system. When you say you're Christian, you kind of throw it out there for the world to know there's an expected level of behavior and ethics that you're going to be held accountable for. We create a stage for what our behavior is expected to be." The Barclays have made living in the world, not of the world, relatively simple by living according to their terms and letting everyone know in a gentle, nonabrasive way what those terms are.

Another close friend, Barbara Barrington Jones, spent many years developing a strong reputation for her knowledge of the fashion and modeling industry. Because of Barbara's expertise, women from all walks of life have consulted with her on how to better themselves both in appearance and in self-confidence. When young ladies involved in pageants seek her out, there are some who are surprised to hear she stresses *spirituality* as one area to develop in becoming a well-rounded person. Barbara has introduced gospel principles to countless women—and they pay her for it! Many of them have felt the Spirit as she has explained the concept of spirituality to them, and as a result, their lives have been changed. "I teach the girls about Heavenly Father and the power of the priesthood, because when they walk out on stage, there is no one left. That's why I go out on a limb. I know they'll be alone and will have only Heavenly Father with them," says Barbara. Though it might be hard to imagine how Barbara could successfully intermingle things of the Spirit with things of the world, she has done so, very successfully.

I too have learned from my own experience that it can be done. In fact, I am convinced that it's possible to dodge the fiery darts of Satan and resist the temptations he makes so glamorous and enticing. At the same time, we can stand as witnesses for God and for the standards he has given us without coming across as stuffy or giving the impression we feel we are better than other people. We are, in fact, commanded to be prepared to explain our beliefs and account for the way we behave. Peter counseled the members of the Church to do this when he said, "But sanctify the Lord God in your hearts: and *be ready always to give an answer* to every man that asketh you a reason of the hope that is in you" (1 Peter 3:15; emphasis added).

We need to live our religion, and when we get an opportunity, we need to be able to *explain* our religion too. We ought to also be willing to risk drawing attention to ourselves or even facing ridicule, if that's what it takes, to be true to our beliefs. Few of us are put in the position of Abinadi, who gave his life defending the Church. Usually it's not like that. But we each come in contact with people who don't know anything about "Mormonism" or who have a lot of misconceptions about the Church.

Some of us are frightened when we think about being put

in that kind of position. We may wonder how, without appearing rude or narrow-minded, we can refuse a drink of alcohol or explain why we shun certain activities. Few of us enjoy being put on the spot like that.

My friend Cathy once wrote me: "It always surprises me how many are afraid to talk about who they are and what they believe. It's never been an issue for me—I've always been proud to be a Mormon, a member of The Church of Jesus Christ of Latter-day Saints. . . . I wouldn't have joined if I didn't have strong feelings like that." And that's the point—to be *proud* (in a humble sort of way!) of who you are and what you stand for. Resist the tendency to be self-conscious or worried about what others might think. I have a favorite quote by Earl Nightingale: "You wouldn't worry so much about what other people thought of you, if you only realized how little they did!" (*Insights,* audiocassette).

The experiences I have chosen to include in this book illustrate awkward situations, challenging circumstances, career-threatening dilemmas, and honest questions that might possibly face the Latter-day Saint who has ventured into the world of "Babylon," which we can define for our purposes in this book as a place, a job, a profession, or a situation in which we are surrounded by those who do not share our LDS values and standards. The experiences I will describe may help you respond to others' questions, challenges, and doubts. These are not the only ways to respond. Undoubtedly, there are a number of ways to handle each situation. In sharing these examples, I am only suggesting that no one need be afraid to be different. Don't hesitate to stand up for the standards of the Church or to declare your membership. If you do so in a spirit of goodwill, with a smile and a sense of humor, you are not likely to offend anyone. The important thing is to never give in to worldly pressures or permit uneducated or crude people to ridicule the things you cherish and hold sacred. If nothing else works, reminding someone who is taunting you that it is politically incorrect to make fun of those who are different will usually quiet them!

In this book I discuss some effective ways to represent the Church while maintaining standards. In doing so, I relate some of my experiences and those of others who have found themselves in a position to explain or demonstrate what Mormons believe. I also share ideas, examples, concepts, and philosophies that might be used in challenging situations. I've also included suggested answers to some of the questions a Latter-day Saint might typically be asked while living and working in the "real" or non-LDS world.

I hope you'll find these experiences and philosophies interesting and that this book will be helpful to you as you face many of the same situations I have faced. A favorite motto is the title of a popular country tune: "You've got to stand for something, or you'll fall for anything." So, regardless of the forum, whether in the White House or a neighbor's home, I believe our duty as members of Christ's church is the same: "To stand as witnesses of God at all times and in all things, and in all places" (Mosiah 18:9).

CHAPTER I

BEACONS IN BABYLON

When my father was much younger, he did a lot of flying as a pilot of small planes in South America. He loves flying, and I grew up hearing about his exciting adventures. I especially loved the story of a beacon light that guided him to safety on a dark and stormy night.

A friend of my dad's had asked Dad to pilot a charter flight for him. Dad was to use his friend's airplane, taking off in daylight and expecting to return before sundown. On the outbound flight, he discovered that the plane's magnetic compass was not working, but he wasn't concerned. After all, he was flying in daylight over familiar terrain.

After arriving at the remote jungle destination, he was delayed for some time, and he wasn't able to take off for the return flight until sundown. He flew into a fast-darkening sky. To make matters worse, a line of thunderstorms boiled up right across his path. The only weather information he had received was based on primitive forecasting methods which had anticipated the front's arrival the following day. He couldn't return to the jungle airstrip because there were no lights there. He suddenly faced a dangerous dilemma.

My father tells the story this way: "I was flying in darkness with a faulty and undependable magnetic compass, and the radio compass began homing in on the nearby electrical thunderstorms instead of the distant home-base radio beacon. . . . Scattered rain became steady rain and a lowering ceiling turned into lowering visibility and increasing turbulence. The unexpected front had a severe wind change that blew me off course and the expected ranch house lights did not appear any longer. I was lucky that I was flying over flat terrain with no hills or mountains or other obstacles."

Dad eventually crossed what he thought must be the big river below him in the darkness. The airport he was seeking was on the river, but he had no way of knowing whether it was upriver or downriver from where he crossed it. There was no light from which to take his bearings—only blackness. Taking a chance, he turned right. A light came into view.

"The most welcome sight I have ever seen was the two-million-candlepower rotating beacon on the top of the airport tower, first visible dimly through the rain and then more and more clearly as I flew towards it. The rotating beacon did not illuminate my path; rather it gave me the needed reference point in the midst of rainy blackness to fly towards a lighted runway and safety" (Robert E. Wells Journal).

The Lord knows that many in the world need only a point of reference in the midst of spiritual darkness, storm, and uncertainty to guide them toward salvation and eternal life. The world yearns for more beacon lights as examples to follow.

There are many ways to live safely *in* the world without being *of* the world. At the Last Supper, the Savior explained to his apostles that they would continue "in the world," though he would soon be leaving them to return to his Father in Heaven (see John 17:11–18). Being in the world—that is, being engaged in mortal life—includes working with and associating with individuals who are not of our faith, who hold very different views and standards from ours, and who may even scoff at the very idea of faith in God.

In the Savior's great Intercessory Prayer at the Last Supper, he asked the Father "not that thou shouldest take them out of the world, but that thou shouldest keep them from the evil" (verse 15). He emphasized that these men of God were "*not of the world,* even as I am not of the world" (John 17:16; emphasis added). The Apostle John's counsel to the early Saints helps us to define what it means to be "*of* the world." This faithful disciple of Christ counseled the Saints to "love not the world, neither the things that are in the world" (1 John 2:15), then reminded them that all that is worldly, including "the lust of the flesh, and the lust of the eyes, and the pride of life, is not of the Father, but is *of the world*" (verse 16; emphasis added).

We do not need to run away from the world or abandon our gospel treasures to live there. Our challenge is to be strong enough and sufficiently prepared to live in Babylon—the worldly, materialistic, pleasure-seeking, valueless environment that surrounds us—while resisting temptation, and in addition we need to work effectively in that arena to bring others to Christ.

The dictionary says a beacon is a signal or a beam emitted by a lighthouse or a radio transmitter for the guidance of ships or aircraft. The sailors or pilots "home in" on the beacon by directing their course toward the signal or beam and moving toward it while taking care to avoid obstacles that lie in the way. A faithful member of the Church living out in the world can be a beautiful example and a point of reference for those

who are drifting without direction. By serving as spiritual beacons, such members can help steer those who are otherwise
lost to the safety found in the welcoming arms of Christ. If we
were all to stay safely at home, huddled in the places where the
Church is fully established and well-known, who then would
be the "beacon lights" in the faraway and dark places?

It can be an exciting spiritual adventure to be out in the
world, where you have to work to not be corrupted by the
world. In fact, contrary to popular belief, some members of the
Church (myself included) have found that in many ways it is
actually easier to live the gospel and insulate their children
from the evils of the world in "the mission field," as we have
traditionally called areas outside Utah, than it is in the center
stakes of Zion! And in my opinion, this is why: In areas of heavy
concentrations of Church members, the levels of commitment
are not quite so black and white as they are in the "mission
field." There may even be more members who live their lives
in the gray areas, because these members seek others with the
same levels of commitment they are comfortable with, and
(again, because of sheer numbers) half-committed members
can always find someone else to share that same spot. In this
way, mediocrity, or an overly casual approach to living the
gospel, sometimes seems completely acceptable. Thus, some
are truly committed, some are occasionally committed according to whether or not Church involvement happens to be con-
venient at the time, and others feel comfortable with little or
no commitment to live the gospel. But many who live and
work out in the world find that our standards are *so* different
from others' standards that we have ample opportunity to see

and define precisely the difference between a committed member of the Church and all others.

I was selected Miss America 1985 in the midst of a very controversial situation. The previous Miss America had been forced to resign because of scandalous pictures that had been published in *Penthouse* magazine. For that year in particular, I lived in full view and scrutiny of the entire world. I was constantly monitored by members of the media who were ready to criticize any discrepancies between my conduct and my LDS standards. Fortunately, this experience was not entirely new to me or to my family. While I was growing up, my family lived for many years in Latin America, where my dad worked for an international bank. There, he was also closely observed by staff, clients, government officials, and members of the foreign diplomatic corps. He was often in a position in which people would have been able to detect any differences between his stated beliefs and the way he lived.

In these and other circumstances, my family and I have often had to stand up for the Church and defend our beliefs. I hope our experiences will help members of the Church who find themselves in similar situations. In today's world, circumstances often take Latter-day Saints inside the boundaries of a world far different from the one the Lord would establish.

I have no doubt we *can* live in such a world without compromising our standards or losing our spirituality. We can compete with the best and often be rewarded for it. But there are decisions that need to be made before we cross the borders into Babylon: How much time do I spend away from my family? Am I willing to avoid working on Sundays? How will I behave in certain social situations?

Certainly, there are some activities, careers, and environments that must be avoided no matter what. It would be foolish to risk everything we hold dear to our heart for a foolhardy confrontation with the evil things of this world. But a courageous and determined Latter-day Saint can operate in most settings and find success without giving up or giving in. It is possible to attend universities, follow a career, or work in a corporate climate where standards of the Church are not generally practiced, and find happiness, success, and recognition at the same time. If your standards are high and your resolve is certain, you can rise above challenges, not only surviving in such places but also thriving and growing. I have found that even with ridicule and temptation on every side, there is no need to compromise or be afraid.

As the number of Church members increases, more and more of us are studying or pursuing careers in the midst of an increasingly challenging environment. Many find themselves competing for positions or salaries with those who have different standards or possibly no standards at all. When advancements, grades, or opportunities seem to depend on our willingness to participate in things that are contrary to our beliefs, our choices become difficult. Too much confrontation will often alienate rather than befriend; too much preaching may frighten away or cause resentment; refusal to participate often comes across as self-righteous and will be misunderstood and labeled as arrogant behavior or a "holier than thou" attitude. But with the help of the Spirit and some good ideas, we can turn every situation to our benefit. The dilemma is that while we cannot hide from differences or entirely ignore them, we must not accept others' vices or adopt their sins.

Survival in these kinds of situations requires balance and maturity. Our goal ought to be to adhere to our beliefs without becoming confrontational, yet at the same time to protect and even defend that which is so valuable to us. Obviously, it's not easy. The delicate balance required of us might seem even too challenging for a seasoned diplomat to handle: To live without offending or alienating others or surrendering to their vices, yet at the same time to attract them to Christ and to our way of living his gospel. It takes diplomacy and tact to be a light to the world. In all of our endeavors, the Lord expects us to stand as his witnesses.

There are many fast-track career opportunities out in the world that can lead to personal and financial success. But even more important than our success is how we conduct our lives. We serve the Lord's cause more effectively when we live our standards in such a way that we can be examples or lights to the world, providing a spiritual model where none was found before and helping those of Father's children who are likely to accept the gospel. I don't believe we serve the Lord when we live as hermits, recluses, or provincial isolationists. How do we know but what the job offer from half a continent away is an opportunity the Lord has prepared so that we can be in a position to share the gospel? We may not wear nametags, but our work can be just as essential as that of the young missionaries who do. The world is full of people who are looking for the truth, for righteousness, and for lofty standards to live. Speaking of our obligations as members of the Church, the Lord says, "There are many yet on the earth among all sects, parties, and denominations, who are blinded by the subtle craftiness of men, whereby they lie in wait to deceive, and who

7

are only kept from the truth because they know not where to find it" (D&C 123:12). Perhaps it is our example that will trigger their interest and serve to introduce them to their divine destiny.

There are many wonderful and sincere people in the world, yet it is likely that in some places not one person in a thousand, or even in a million, will have ever heard of The Church of Jesus Christ of Latter-day Saints or of the plan of salvation. Many of these good people are honestly looking for happiness and ways to improve their lives, but the way of Christ is unknown to them, and many have minds clouded over by misconceptions and doubt. If we are in the right place, we can be the beacon they are searching for.

Some time ago I was in Aspen, Colorado, filming a television show on the sport of snowboarding. During a lull in the shooting, I was sitting in a Snowcat with the operator. As we visited, he said, "So, how many other wives does your husband have?"

At first I thought he was kidding and I laughed. Then I saw that he was serious. He actually believed that Mormons still practice polygamy!

Still smiling, I said, "Do you mind if I bring you up to date?"

I explained to him that some Mormons used to live the practice of polygamy, but that since 1890, when our prophet and president issued the Manifesto, plural marriage had been abolished in the Church. I told him that if he ever met a polygamist, he could be certain that person wasn't a member of our church.

Then the Snowcat operator asked, "What about the armed

standoffs between the FBI and those religious fanatics in Utah? Are those people Mormons?"

I was happy to explain to him that they weren't, that the Church has nearly nine million members all over the world, and that we are not a cult or a sect. He wasn't the least bit offended by my explanation. In fact, he said he was glad to meet someone who could set him straight. Perhaps someday he'll have further opportunity to discuss the gospel with someone else, when he won't have any misconceptions to bog him down.

As members of the Lord's church, we have been charged by the Savior to help guide all of Heavenly Father's children back to him. He said, "Hold up your light that it may shine unto the world. Behold I am the light which ye shall hold up" (3 Nephi 18:24). There are two ways to spread the light—by the candle or by the mirror that reflects it.

BYU professor Robert L. Millet writes, "In a world which is too often shrouded in uncertainty and doubt, the Light of Life [the Savior] bids us to let our light shine, to stand as beacons in the storms of the night, and to certify our discipleship. . . . Discipleship involves standing out from the generality of mankind and standing up for what is true and right and good. . . . Christ is the Light. We are at best lamps, dim reflections of him. But to the degree that the light of his Spirit shines in our souls, to the degree that his image is in our countenances, to the degree that our good works motivate others to sing the song of redeeming love and glorify God, we are in the line of our duty as disciples" (*An Eye Single to the Glory of God* [Salt Lake City: Deseret Book Company, 1991], pp. 47, 50).

In the moments after I was crowned Miss America, I admit

that I was a bit overwhelmed as I recognized the duty I had before me to be a beacon. Actually, I didn't feel like a beacon at all. I felt the whole world had their spotlight turned on *me*, and, yes, I was fearful. Maybe I was a little bit like David Whitmer, to whom the Lord once said, "Behold, I say unto you, David, that you have feared man and have not relied on me for strength as you ought" (D&C 30:1). But it was the Lord's words from that very section (verse 11), words I had read and memorized the week before, that helped me overcome my initial bout with fear: "And your whole labor shall be in Zion, with all your soul, . . . yea, you shall ever open your mouth in my cause, not fearing what man can do, for I am with you." *Not fearing what man can do, for I am with you!* To me, those are powerful words of support and encouragement. Hey, knowing that, I can do anything and withstand any pressure! I recall some advice I later heard from our bishop's wife when Bob and I were living in Massachusetts. She once told the youth of our ward that there's no need to fear standing up for your beliefs when you understand this simple formula:

One + God = the Majority

That idea has stuck with me ever since. I like being on the winning team. With God on our side, we are in the majority, and by disregarding fear, we are then able to serve the Lord as beacons, whether we are missionaries, students, businesspeople, or professionals.

TAKING RESPONSIBILITY

A ll my life, it seems, I have walked through countless doors of opportunity to serve as an example in a visible way. As a young child, and then as a teenager, I lived in Latin American countries where I fervently hope that I did my best to reflect the truth that is the gospel of Jesus Christ. I am sure that there were times when I faltered, when I could have done better to live as I believed. But as I look back on my unique twentieth year, I see that it was at that time in my life that I finally felt responsible for how I *represented* the Church, not just passively believed in it. Up until then, I simply felt grateful for my testimony of the true gospel of Jesus Christ and hoped I might help others find that same happiness. It felt a little strange to actually feel responsible for how others might view the Church as a whole. I worried that I might say or do something wrong that would turn people away.

Allow me to share the sequence of events that put me in such a visible position, and the dilemma my parents faced leading up to it as they wondered whether or not one of the scholarship routes I had chosen, the Miss America scholarship pageant, was a good choice—both as a tool to better myself and as an opportunity to represent everything that mattered most to me.

During the years of Dad's professional career, he worked

for the prestigious international Citibank. He had always assumed that he would be able to finance the college educations of his seven children, even if we chose to attend expensive private institutions. Mom and Dad had struggled to pay for their own schooling, and they were determined to help us kids go as far as we wanted to obtain career-focused training. They focused on setting aside funds that would enable us to go on missions and complete our education.

One of the most important things our parents did was to emphasize the steps we needed to take in order to qualify for acceptance to a major university. We were taught the value of good grades, language training, community service, and music appreciation. That kind of training turned out to be good for each of us.

Then, suddenly, Dad's career was interrupted by a call to preside over a mission for three years. He and Mom considered that a great honor, and they were eager and happy to accept the assignment. The bank generously offered to give Dad a three-year leave of absence. I was only four years old at the time.

As promised, the bank got in touch with Dad just before the end of their mission in Mexico, welcoming him back and offering him a position that was much better than my parents had anticipated after being away for three years. The way seemed open for Dad to get back onto the financial "fast track."

But then Dad was asked to follow a different track altogether—a track that would eventually lead to his becoming a General Authority. President N. Eldon Tanner of the First Presidency asked Dad if he would consider taking an administrative position at Church headquarters. President Tanner said the Church needed someone with international experience in managing money and supervising people on a large scale.

The position the Church offered him was at a much lower salary than his bank position, with none of the executive "perks" Citibank had provided. President Tanner was frank in saying that what he was extending was not a "call to serve," but rather, only a job offer. Moreover, the position was somewhat experimental, and Dad might be let go "with or without cause," if things didn't work out. To make the decision harder for my parents, Dad had just one more year to go with the bank to qualify for vested retirement and a substantial pension.

My parents took the matter to the Lord and received the distinct impression that this was a test to see if they really loved God more than "mammon." Were they laying up treasures in heaven or on earth? Were they willing to make the sacrifice in order to serve in the Lord's kingdom? They knew that the Lord always gives compensating blessings, so, acting on faith, they made the decision to accept the Church position. By doing so, Dad knew he had "burned his bridges" at the bank. He knew that after turning down their offer, he would never again, because of his age, be able to return to them or hook up with any other major international organization.

We moved to Salt Lake City when I was in second grade. My parents invested their entire savings in a home. We had to adjust to a lower standard of living than we had enjoyed when Dad was an international banker. For the first time in our lives, the older children were expected to go out and get jobs to earn spending money. I don't remember, but my older brothers and sisters say that our parents also explained to us that they would no longer be able to help finance our college educations. Each of us would need to either work for the grades and qualifications that would earn scholarships or perhaps enter the military to finance our education.

Mom had worked her way through college by studying a year, then working and saving for a few years, then going back to college to finish. Dad had joined the Navy to finance his four-year education. Naturally, they figured we could do the same and be the better for it.

By the time I was a junior in high school, I was saving money for both a mission (I had been building a mission fund ever since I was ten) and for college. It was easy to see I had better be working toward getting a scholarship of one kind or another, and I kept my eyes open for scholarship opportunities.

By the time I was ready to graduate from high school, I had earned a dean's scholarship to Brigham Young University. Earlier during my senior year in high school, I had entered the Utah Junior Miss competition, where I had earned $11,000 in a cash scholarship. This kind of scholarship could be applied toward just about anything that was school-related, so I was grateful to be able to receive financial assistance through that program.

Then, during my freshman year at BYU, while looking for further ways to finance my college career, I entered the Miss Utah pageant. I was chosen as second runner-up, and I won additional scholarship help. The Miss Utah pageant is part of the larger Miss America pageant, which was originally conceived by the Atlantic City Chamber of Commerce as a way to extend the tourist season at that beach resort for a few weeks beyond Labor Day in the fall. The pageant has since grown to be the largest scholarship foundation for women in the world.

When I entered the Miss Utah competition for the second time, I asked my parents if they would support me. Dad was by this time a General Authority, having been called to serve in the First Quorum of the Seventy about five years after our move to Salt Lake City. My parents were primarily concerned about the effect the pageant would have on me. They wanted to know more about the conditions, chaperons, contest rules, judging, and the general environment at the competition. Of course, we had financial concerns too: the purpose of my involvement was not to spend money on clothes but to earn more for school, so my expenses needed to be kept to a minimum.

My parents and I talked to other LDS contestants who had won the state contest and gone on to complete in the Miss America pageant in Atlantic City in prior years. It turned out that each of the previous Miss Utahs, along with their parents with whom we spoke, felt good about the experience. Mom and Dad studied the whole situation very carefully and became convinced that the pageant officials were moral, decent, proper business executives and family-oriented people.

After considering all the aspects of the contest and making it a matter of prayer, my parents and I felt good about my entering the Miss Utah pageant. Having made that decision, it became something of a family project.

To save money, I borrowed a dressy suit to wear during the judges' interviews, and for the swimsuit competition, I used a modest blue suit that I already had. After I won Miss Utah, a dear friend of our family contributed to my wardrobe fund, which helped us considerably. Even so, I am sure that mine was the lowest-budget wardrobe worn by any contestant that year.

I didn't know the full extent of it at the time, but my dad

was being subjected to considerable pressure from some well-meaning friends who were concerned about my entering the Miss America pageant. Some warned that if I won I could easily be corrupted by the attendant fame and fortune and become vain and self-centered. One of Dad's friends expressed concern that my participation might somehow discredit the Church and even quoted from Isaiah: "The daughters of Zion are haughty, and walk with stretched forth necks and wanton eyes, walking and mincing as they go, and making a tinkling with their feet: . . . [with] bracelets, . . . and the earrings, the rings, and nose jewels, the changeable suits of apparel, and the mantles, and the wimples, and the crisping pins" (Isaiah 3:16, 19–22). Others wondered if my parents weren't "flirting with Babylon" and perhaps putting my reputation or character in jeopardy. We were warned that some of the Brethren would surely object to a daughter of a General Authority entering a "bathing beauty contest." Still others speculated that the experience might cause a change in my personality or contribute to some lowering of my standards.

In response to these kinds of concerns, Dad wrote in his journal: "True, this risk is very real, but Helen and I felt that we knew our daughter Sharlene well enough to know that she would not succumb to the ways of the world. Beneath whatever concerns might have occurred to us or were suggested to us, we were aware of all the good that might be accomplished if an active LDS girl were to win the title of Miss America. We had lived out in the international world where we [had seen] what great missionary work could be done by even one person who lived their religion as an example."

In the midst of this controversy, something happened that

came as if in answer to our prayers and concerns. The presidency of the Quorum of the Seventy insisted that Dad take the week off to be with me and Mom in Atlantic City, even though they understood that my parents would be allowed to be with me only a few minutes each day. Dad's colleagues assured him it was important for him to go. They said to him: "You should be there with her. Your daughter will be representing the state of Utah and the Church as well as your family." That vote of confidence and support meant a lot to all of us. Then, on the final night of competition, these wonderful men lent their further support by sending me a telegram wishing me well.

Several months after the competition, I was surprised to be invited to a banquet in my honor that was held on the top floor of the Church Office Building. President Spencer W. Kimball was not well enough at that point to attend social functions, but Dad had the privilege of sitting next to Sister Kimball. During the course of the meal, she told him how proud she was about my winning the Miss America title and crown. Dad told me later he couldn't help but ask Sister Kimball, "How does President Kimball feel about all this?" She answered, "Sharlene has brought so much credit to the Church by speaking out about her standards that Spencer feels very happy about her success."

It wasn't until later—after the competition—that I learned the full extent of some of the pressures Dad was feeling over my participation in this pageant. It was wonderful to learn that a prophet of the Lord approved of what I had done. In fact, that endorsement meant more to me than any of the world's approval. I was grateful too for the support of my parents. And during the competition I felt I was being watched and judged by an unseen audience. I felt a responsibility that is still with me to live up to what my Church leaders and teachers, my parents, and my Heavenly Father expect of me. I believe all members of the Church share the same duty and responsibility to live as good examples in all that we do and say, to be beacons of light to someone out there who needs us.

A CHANCE TO BLOW THE TRUMPET

F ew of us ever get a chance to "blow the trumpet" and tell the world what we believe. In the aftermath of the Miss America pageant in 1984, I had an opportunity to frequently describe our standards and explain our religion. It's a bit scary to literally stand before the world and answer any questions the media people dare ask. As I went into my first press conference, I wondered almost the same things I had wondered my first day of junior high or high school: *Will they approve of me, like me, accept me? Am I going to be sophisticated enough to satisfy their expectations? What kinds of questions will I be asked?*

To be honest, when I first walked into the room and saw it full of media "vultures" who looked as though they wanted to pick me apart, I began to doubt myself a little. I wondered if it was going to be necessary to expose all the things that would make me appear strange, out of touch, and "squeaky clean." Part of me wanted to be accepted, to be seen as "with it," sophisticated, the quintessential modern woman. But it only took a moment to put that temptation aside. I realized that what I was feeling was fear—fear of what they might say or write about me. Fear that I would be perceived as too different to represent the young women of America. Fear of their opinions. And I didn't even know them! I should have been far more concerned about the opinions of those I care about most: my family, my Heavenly Father, even myself.

Even though I was fearful, I was at the same time grateful—grateful that at twenty years of age I had already determined exactly who I was. So, though I was initially nervous and momentarily intimidated, I thought of the scripture I mentioned earlier that had impressed me so much before I went to Atlantic City that I had committed it to memory: "You shall ever open your mouth in my cause, not fearing what man can do, for I am with you" (D&C 30:11). As I reviewed the scripture in my mind, I knew exactly why I had been impressed to memorize those words. I felt peace and purpose, courage and confidence, knowing God was on my side, and I was on his.

I want to include in this book my father's unique perspective on the pageant, the final evening of the competition, and my first press conference. Please forgive Dad for his biased point of view and what may look like an attempt to make me look good. He and Mom were understandably excited and very proud. The events of the competition and the press conference did unfold just as he describes them, but I honestly feel that almost any other LDS young woman who had grown up in a home where the Church was loved and missionary work was emphasized would have responded in much the same way as I did. Now, for Dad's version of the Atlantic City experience:

"Before Sharlene left home to fly to Atlantic City to represent the great state of Utah in the Miss America Scholarship Pageant, she asked for a father's blessing. . . . I did not bless her to win, nor did she ask me to bless her to that end. I simply blessed her with health and strength; with protection against harm, accident, or illness; and with the ability to do her very best, to make new friends, to represent the Church well, and to be a proper example. I also blessed her to be able to respond effectively to missionary-type opportunities; to be calm and in control of the situations in which she might find herself; to sing and play the harp to the very best of her ability; and, using a phrase from the scriptures that I had included in family blessings previously, I blessed her that she might 'have angels round about her' at all times to help as needed.

"We were not allowed to accompany our daughter to Atlantic City. The pageant rules specified that each state send an official chaperon to help and support the state winner, and to see that all the rules, such as no dates and no boyfriends, were followed. Parents and members of the contestant's family were invited to attend the week's activities, but contact was limited to a few moments each evening in the lobby of a hotel. We had time only for a quick hug and a word of encouragement.

"The night of the finals arrived at last. It was Saturday, and all day long the radio, TV, and newspapers had been filled with speculation about who of the fifty contestants would be in the final ten. There would be worldwide television coverage of that evening's concluding events and the crowning of a new Miss America. Never in the history of the Atlantic City pageant had interest and speculation been as keen. The viewing audience would be an all-time record—and with good reason. Never before had the reigning Miss America been so publicly disgraced as was the young woman who *should* have been ending her reign. She was a beautiful and talented girl with deep spiritual roots; however, she had made a fateful mistake by posing for nude photographs before being named Miss America.

When the photographs were published, the story flashed around the world, and she was forced to resign. The first runner-up finished the year in her place.

"Immediately, a debate broke out in the press. Many editors wrote that it was unfair for the pageant committee to treat this lovely young woman so severely just because she had acted imprudently. After all, they reasoned, we are no longer a puritanical, Victorian society. . . . Feminine nudity is part of art. That kind of liberal rationalization was met head-on by other editors who held that Miss America should be a role model for all the young women of our country and that she had an obligation, both by written contract and by tradition, to exemplify modesty, virtue, and femininity. The pageant officials pointed to the contract the winner had signed, in which she had agreed to do nothing that would embarrass the pageant.

"All this accomplished, however, was to stir up controversy and public interest in the competition—the year in which Sharlene was an overlooked contender—overlooked by all except a few friends and family members.

"As we took our seats that Saturday night, we dared hope that since Sharlene had been a preliminary winner, she might be one of the ten finalists. That was great, exciting news. If it was true that she was a finalist, it meant that, against all odds, she had been brought to the attention of the judges.

"The lights went on, the huge curtain opened wide, the orchestra filled the vast auditorium with music, the crowd applauded as the contestants filed in, and the show began. After the parade of all fifty beautiful young women, the moment finally arrived for Gary Collins to announce the names of the ten finalists. As he read the names, I was so nervous that it seemed to me he had already named ten and had not mentioned Miss Utah. I was sure she was not included . . . but, then, he announced: 'MISS UTAH—SHARLENE WELLS!' She was in! Even if she hadn't made the final cut, it had all been worthwhile. All fifty girls were beautiful, talented, intelligent, athletic, poised, feminine, and qualified to represent their state and the nation. How could the judges pick only one! It was going to be a heart-stopper for us.

"I must explain something. The Miss America pageant is not a 'beauty contest.' It is more like a heptathlon. In an Olympic heptathlon, the winner is not necessarily the highest jumper, the fastest swimmer, the speediest runner, etc. Rather, the winner is the one with the highest number of overall points.

"Likewise, Miss America is selected on the basis of the total number of points accumulated in the several areas of competition. In the 1984/1985 contest, the formula was: performing talent, 50 percent; judge's interview, 20 percent; physical fitness, 15 percent; and evening gown, 15 percent.

"In Sharlene's year, as a result of the resignation of her predecessor, I believe there was also an unmentioned but critical consideration: morality, virtue, and unquestioned conduct.

"Because of the way the competition was weighted, the talent segment was most important. We were sure that was in Sharlene's favor because her performance—singing a hauntingly beautiful Spanish song while accompanying herself on the Paraguayan harp—would permit her to showcase her talent effectively. But, then, all the young women were very talented, and they all performed at professional levels.

"In the end, our Sharlene succeeded in captivating the

judges. Our twenty-year-old daughter was crowned Miss America. We clapped and cried and hugged each other. I completely lost my reserved composure.

"But the best part was yet to come. In a few minutes she would have her first chance to use her celebrity status to speak out and declare her standards and beliefs.

"Not far from the huge performing stage and the ramp on which Sharlene had just walked as the newly crowned Miss America was an equally cavernous room where she conducted her first press conference. The pageant officials led Charlie [Dad's nickname for me] into the room, already packed to standing room only, and took her up front to a rostrum crowded with microphones. We were standing in the back of the room, off to one side. The room was filled with reporters and photographers from many parts of the world. It was a chaotic scene, filled with people jostling for position, noise, flashing cameras, and bright Kleig floodlights. It was a setting that was more than a little intimidating. Due to the unprecedented scandal surrounding the previous year's winner, interest had been magnified, and the crowd in that room and the world outside were all anxious to discover what kind of young woman had just become the new Miss America.

"The officials who had escorted Sharlene into the room brought her to the podium and simply left her there. The pack of reporters began shouting questions at her. Startled by the unruly mob before her, Sharlene looked over at the officials. No one moved to help her calm the chaos. They were apparently as surprised as she was. Being a take-charge kind of guy, I started to go up front to help her bring the scene to order, when she did it herself.

"She raised her arms and called out to them, 'Be quiet . . . be quiet, please!' They quieted down. She motioned with her hands, saying, 'Please, sit down . . . sit down, please.'

"After they were seated, she said to them, 'Now, if you'll raise your hands, I'll call on you.' She turned to her right, pointed to a reporter on the front row, and with a smile asked politely, 'What is your question?'

"The fellow was surprised. He gulped and then asked a short question. She answered it, then turned to her left and pointed to another reporter and asked, 'Now, what is your question?'

"Again, the guy stammered, finally found a question, and she answered it. A murmur of surprise and approval rippled through that sophisticated crowd. One close to us turned to another reporter and exclaimed, 'Wow. I've never seen a girl take charge like this before!' Another one within earshot declared, 'She sure comes on strong. . . . We've got a real winner this time!'

"She had control of that unruly mob, had put them in their place and brought order out of chaos—sort of as though they were Primary children and she was their teacher. But our proudest moment of all was next to come.

"Sharlene signaled to a reporter seated out in the middle. He asked what I thought was a pointless question. 'Miss America,' he said, very respectfully, 'how is this going to change your life?'

"I thought everyone knew that all fifty state winners sign a contract that should they win, they become the property of the pageant for one year. They are obligated to drop out of college, leave home, not date anyone, and spend the entire year traveling across the country making prearranged appearances. They do so in the company of an assigned, mature, strong, motherly chaperon. Winning meant that Sharlene would have to drop out of BYU and would lose her housing and registration deposits. Thinking of that, I was suddenly chagrined that she would lose several hundred dollars, forgetting that she had just won a $25,000 scholarship, a red convertible automobile, and a year's contract that would provide six digits of income for her.

"Thinking of all those things, I thought the answer to the reporter's question was obvious. How is this going to change your life? From that moment on she would be a celebrity and would average staying in five different hotels per week for the next year. But Sharlene saw it in a different light. She recognized an opportunity to say something important.

"One of the rules of public relations is that if the reporters don't ask the right question, answer with the right information anyway. So she looked at him, smiled beautifully, and responded, 'This is not going to change my life a bit. I have always tried to live my standards twenty-four hours a day, seven days a week, fifty-two weeks a year. This is not going to change my life at all.'

"It was a different answer than I expected and different apparently from what anyone else expected. The reporter who had asked the question was still on his feet, and although they had all been told they would be allowed only one question, he blurted out, 'Tell us . . . what *are* your standards?'

"Smiling radiantly, Sharlene replied in a strong, clear voice: 'My standards are no drugs, no alcohol, no tobacco, no coffee or tea, no sex before marriage, no sex outside of marriage, and to live the Judeo-Christian ethics to the best of my ability.'

"A loud murmur of amazement and nods of approval swept through the hall. Reporters and TV cameramen looked at each other in surprise. Many had their heads buried in hurried note taking. People near us were turning to strangers next to them and saying such things as 'I've been covering the pageant for twenty-five years, and this is the sharpest winner I've ever seen . . . She sounds more like a lawyer than a twenty-year-old . . . We've never had a Miss America like this before . . . ' and on and on.

"Helen and I were thrilled she had won, but we were now becoming aware that our prayers were being answered and the blessing given to Sharlene before coming to Atlantic City was being fulfilled and magnified in a way far beyond what we had ever anticipated. Now she was really doing some missionary work. She had been given a way to become a powerful spokesperson.

"The next incident was even more thrilling. A question was asked, 'Miss America, have you ever posed in the nude?' The blunt inquiry drew a nervous laugh from the crowd, but Charlie handled it with her normal, natural humor: 'Me? A Mormon girl from Utah? You've gotta be kidding!' The audience roared with laughter. She had them eating out of her hand.

"I thought the next question was totally out of line. Helen and I were amazed that anyone would think to ask our daughter something like this, but in retrospect, she probably opened herself up for it by her previous statements. The brash and insensitive question was 'Miss America, you say your standards include no sex before marriage and no sex outside of marriage. Are you, then, a virgin?'

"Sharlene answered with total candor and self-assurance: 'Yes, sir, and proud to be one! Next question.'

"She faced those hard-boiled, skeptical, and worldly journalists—some of the most difficult people in the world to impress—on their own turf, back East, with honesty and sincerity; and she came out of the encounter with their respect and affection.

"One seasoned writer who represented a very old and prestigious newspaper, a man who had a religious background himself, sought us out and said admiringly, 'I have been fasting and praying that a young woman would be selected this year who could redeem the standards of the pageant and help it recuperate from the damage done last year. Thank you for raising such a daughter. . . . My prayers have been answered.' He moved off before we could get his name.

"Newspapers all over the world reported the uniqueness of the new Miss America, but our favorite headline came from Switzerland and simply said: 'MORMON GIRL RESCUES AMERICA'S MORALITY.' We were so grateful that our daughter was in a position to be an instrument in the hands of the Lord and to be a beacon light in behalf of virtue and morality.

"Of course, the world had to have its fun. There were those who ridiculed her standards and belittled her squeaky-clean image. Bob Hope got off three one-liners about her during that week. He declared on national television, 'The new Miss America is so religious she even has stained glass in her compact.' Then he quipped, 'The new Miss America is so pure, seven dwarfs have been seen following her around.' And my favorite was the one where he said, 'The new Miss America is so modest she couldn't use the swimsuit she brought from Utah . . . (pause) . . . It had a hole in the knee!'

"My favorite cartoon on the subject of her win showed the devil down in the lower regions of the Inferno. An imp brought the bad news to Lucifer, who, when he was told of her virtue, was full of consternation. But what really sent old Satan into a tailspin was the news that 'she even plays the harp!'

"We received hundreds of letters of congratulations from all over the world. People were thrilled. They thanked us for raising a daughter who had the courage to stand up for her standards and beliefs. Even parents who were not members of the Church told us Sharlene's stand had made it easier for them to talk to their own daughters about living a morally clean life. Sharlene had made it fashionable to behave modestly, to live a virtuous life, and had shown that it could all be done without appearing to be a prude.

"One woman reporter asked her, in a genial tone, 'Why do you always talk about morality?' Sharlene's answer was open, direct, and unwavering. 'You reporters ask the questions . . . I just answer them. You are the ones who seem to be interested in my views on the subject.' The reporter agreed and respectfully continued the interview.

"A few of the tabloids could not believe that Sharlene was actually that squeaky clean. They sent reporters to Utah to dig for dirt. They interviewed her roommates, friends, and any young man who claimed to have dated her. One of those reporters was asked why no articles were printed against her. His answer amused us and was a great compliment to her and to the standards of the Church. He said, 'Naw . . . she's too boring.' We are happy the tabloids felt that way.

"We are grateful, too, that our daughter was able to stand as a witness of God at all times, and in all things, and in all places (see Mosiah 18:9). She truly had been placed in a position to be a light to others" (here and elsewhere, I have quoted from my father's personal journal, with his permission).

DRESSING MODESTLY

When I was eighteen years old, I entered my first pageant. First of all, as strange as it sounds, imagining myself being crowned Miss Anything was not one of my childhood dreams. As a young girl, I was plain and simple—a tomboy. But as a senior at Skyline High School in Salt Lake City, I was attracted to the Utah Junior Miss pageant for a very good reason—it offered scholarships!

Besides, it wasn't really a "pageant" in the sense that I had always thought of one. It was actually a scholarship competition that required senior high school young women to submit resumes and essays, be interviewed, and demonstrate talents on stage for the judges to critique. Contestants were also judged on their scholastic achievements—15 percent of each girl's score was based solely on grade-point average, test scores, and the difficulty of courses taken. (Today, it is 20 percent.) In fact, in an effort to reflect more accurately what the competition was all about, the name had been changed to "Utah's Young Woman of the Year" for a while, until such confusion resulted that the original name of the program was again used.

This was hardly a glamorous event, and for those girls who did confuse it with such and showed up in their beaded gowns—well, they didn't make it very far in the competition.

This is a program geared toward the girl who never really thought about being in pageants.

I didn't know much about these kinds of events anyway. I had never watched pageants while I was growing up, partly because we lived in South America during much of my young life. In fact, I had never seen the entire Miss America pageant until I was actually in it. I really didn't know what to expect, and, to be quite honest, I thought I was way out of my league by even signing up for this Utah Junior Miss competition.

At first, I assumed it was like all those other pageants I had heard about, where the contestants had to wear swimsuits and revealing gowns and makeup. But I was quickly assured that I wouldn't have to compete in a swimsuit or wear glamorous, sexy clothing. So, in this initial step in the journey that would take me ultimately to the Miss America title, modesty wasn't a problem. The question simply never arose.

Just a few months after returning from America's Junior Miss finals in Mobile, Alabama, my mom showed me an ad in a Salt Lake newspaper inviting young women to compete in the Miss Salt Lake Valley pageant—a Miss Utah/Miss America preliminary competition. I still didn't know much about pageants, nor did I have much interest in them, so I didn't even know there was a difference between Miss America and Miss USA. All I knew was that contestants in both had to wear swimsuits, and that was something I wasn't sure I would feel comfortable doing.

I nearly decided to ignore the notice, but Mom did a little more checking and found that, yes, there was a swimsuit competition in the Miss Salt Lake Valley pageant, held in private rather than on stage in front of an audience, and that the swimsuit segment only counted for 15 percent of the points and that 50 percent was awarded in the category of talent. This was a scholarship pageant, pretty much along the lines of the Utah Junior Miss program. That part caught my interest. After all, I had just won a significant amount of scholarship money playing my Paraguayan harp, so why not give it another try?

I was still a bit nervous about the swimsuit part, though. I know Dad was *really* nervous about it. As a member of the First Quorum of the Seventy, he wondered if a Mormon girl, especially a General Authority's daughter, should be seen in a public "bathing beauty" competition. When Mom explained how that part of the pageant would be conducted, I think he felt better. We were told that the judges would evaluate the contestants with regard to overall fitness and not physical measurements. I decided that at least I wouldn't embarrass myself—I had always been active in sports and outdoor activities. I was physically fit, so I felt okay about it.

But I did worry about being modest if I had to compete in a swimsuit—even in semiprivacy. I decided to read up on the rules of the Miss America program regarding the kind of swimsuit that could be worn in competition. I found that the leg of the suit couldn't be cut too high, and the top couldn't be cut too low—in fact, the more I thought about it, the more I realized I might have trouble even finding a swimsuit in the stores that would be modest enough for this! I talked to my parents and we decided that the Miss America pageant was in fact based upon high ideals. The organizers of the competition seemed to be looking for attributes that had less to do with physical beauty than with talent, poise, and intelligence. Physical fitness was just part of the mix, and not the major part at that. I reasoned that if Olympic swimmers could go on national television in a suit more revealing than the one I would have to wear, well, then it was a part of the competition I could accept.

With that worry out of the way, I turned my attention to the next question of modesty. Nearly all the beautiful dresses I had seen were either strapless, barely strapped, off-the-shoulder, or cut extremely low—none of which met with my parents' approval. I have to admit, I sure liked the way those kinds of dresses looked on me. They made me feel grown-up and sophisticated. But I knew Mom and Dad were right. I was not in this to promote my exterior—my appearance and wardrobe—as much as I was to project my interior—my personality, talents, and values.

So, for my first dress, I ended up getting an emerald green chiffon halter dress *with a cape,* which Mom and Dad and I agreed was not to be worn without the cape.

After winning Miss Salt Lake Valley at age nineteen, I competed in Orem, Utah, for the Miss Utah pageant. In this competition I learned a lesson the hard way. I quickly decided that I couldn't win unless my dress looked a bit more like the dresses being worn by all the other sixty-three contestants—which, of course, meant losing the cape. Right before going on stage, in a moment of weakness, I decided to go on without it. When the spotlight fell on me, suddenly I felt really bare, and I knew I didn't feel good about my decision. I was sure my parents in the audience were having similar feelings. I didn't feel "sexy" at all. Then and there, I decided that if I ever did this sort of thing again, I would stick with a more modest dress.

I was selected the second runner-up to Miss Utah, which in my mind was practically like winning. I hadn't thought I could even get *that* high with so many outstanding, talented, and attractive young ladies in the competition that year. I felt so good about my results, including some scholarship money, that I had no inclination to try again the next year to see if I could do better. I had become involved pretty much on a whim, and now I was ready to take my life in another direction. Even though it felt foreign to me—a tomboy—to walk in high heels and wear rhinestone earrings, it was, in a way, a lot of fun to get all dressed up *and* have someplace to go. But I was ready to try something else.

Soon after the pageant, I received a call that, as trite as it may sound, changed my life. It was Brent Yorgason, who had been on the panel of judges, and he told me that he had been asked by the other judges to call me and find out if I was planning on entering the pageant again next year. I replied that I didn't think I would. He then asked me if my parents and I would be willing to come to his office for a little chat.

Later in the week, we did go to meet Brother Yorgason, and I remember feeling both in awe and yet at ease in his presence. We sat down, and he began to tell me that the judges felt this was not the right year for me, that I was too young and needed at least one more year of performing experience in order to compete—and *win*—in Atlantic City. That surprised me—to hear that they thought I could win Miss America after I had just lost Miss Utah! Brother Yorgason then spoke of my mission as Miss America and of my unique opportunity to represent the gospel of Jesus Christ, the standards we hold high, and the beliefs we hold sacred. For a few minutes there, I almost felt as if I were being given a calling and it was up to me whether or not I would accept it. I told him I would give it another try, not so much because I believed I could win Miss America, but rather because he and the other judges did. And I knew he was right about the chance of a great missionary opportunity.

The next year rolled around and I was a whole lot older and wiser at twenty years of age. Since it had been so difficult to find a ready-made evening gown that was both glamorous and modest, my parents agreed it would be best to have a dress made. Except maybe for the beads, even the pioneers would have felt okay about the style we chose. It was long, of course, with long sleeves, and the only skin showing was on my hands, my face, and a *bit* of lower leg (to make walking easier). And to make the dress "competition worthy," my mom (and on occasion, even my dad) spent hours and hours sewing tiny beads on by hand. If we had bought the gown ready-made, it would have easily cost close to two thousand dollars!

In that dress I felt very regal, and that was half the battle. Before I could convince the judges, I had to convince myself that I could project myself in something other than jeans and sneakers. Wearing that dress with all those beads reflecting any available light, I felt not only confident but even a little bit glamorous. And I hadn't had to show any skin to achieve the effect.

So the second time I competed in the Miss Utah pageant, I was armed and ready—not necessarily to win, but more importantly, not to back down on myself or compromise my game plan. When I walked on the stage on that final night, I felt calm and assured because I knew I had the right dress on and that I hadn't made any compromises.

It was June 1984 when I won Miss Utah. I had the rest of

that summer to determine what kind of image I wanted to project in Atlantic City, where I would compete in the Miss America contest. What did I want my clothes to say about me? Up until that point, I had never been very fashion-conscious. My main concerns had been simple things: *Do I have a clean shirt to wear that at least won't clash with my pants?* and *Should I wear gold or silver earrings with what I have on?* My system hadn't been the least bit complicated.

But now I had to organize a complete wardrobe, one that would be fashionable, yet unique; stylish, but not outlandish. And, above all, it had to be modest.

In a way, it was fortunate for me that that was the year the pageant was trying to recover somewhat from a scandal. As my dad noted earlier, the reigning Miss America had resigned after some revealing photos of her were published in *Penthouse* magazine. As a result, many of the contestants dressed fairly conservatively during the activities and the competition—feeling perhaps it would be impressive to the judges and pageant officials. I felt certain no one would tease me for wearing modest clothes. In fact, that year it was actually "in" to be conservative. Imagine that!

We decided that, for Atlantic City, I would need a new swimsuit. We searched through the catalogs and stores, even in neighboring states. We couldn't find anything that was high enough where a swimsuit is often low, or low enough where a swimsuit is sometimes too high. Mom finally found a young woman who made me a modest, white satin, 1940ish, Betty Grable—style swimsuit that met our standards.

A lot of time and thought went into the selection of the dress I would be wearing in the evening gown competition. My traveling companion, Rebecca (Beckie) Simpson, remembered being impressed by one of the dresses worn by Audrey Hepburn in the movie *My Fair Lady*. Beckie suggested we watch the film, and when Miss Hepburn, in the role of Eliza Doolittle, descended the stairs to go to the ball, wearing an elegant, classic white gown, Beckie stopped the tape and said, "That's it! That's the dress you should wear!"

We studied the dress—it *was* quite modest—but at first, I thought it might be too old-fashioned. It did have a lot of class, though, and that's what I wanted to convey to the audience and the judges. So we worked with the look. We had a dressmaker modify the pattern somewhat to make the dress more contemporary, and after a few rough drafts, I felt good about it.

When I arrived in Atlantic City and saw the thousand-dollar dresses being unpacked by all the other contestants, I suddenly wasn't so sure about my modest dress. But when I remembered how uncomfortable I had been on the Miss Utah stage when I had removed my green chiffon cape, I thought to myself, *You know, at least I won't have to worry about whether too much is showing or if a strap might break. I will feel perfectly comfortable on stage.*

And I did feel right at home on that enormous stage in front of 21,000 people in the audience and over 100 million viewers on TV. It was a great feeling to have firmly decided what kind of image I wanted to project. That image, very simply, was of the kind of young woman I had always hoped to become by setting all those goals in my *Personal Progress* book when I was a Beehive, Mia Maid, and Laurel. The decision I had made to stay true to those principles gave me confidence and complete assurance.

It didn't matter that I wasn't the most glamorous or even the prettiest one on that stage. I was so at peace knowing that all those adjectives are, well, just adjectives. Accessories, if you will. And like accessories, they are superficial. So, when faced with the alternative, I recognized that really the only alternative I could feel good about was to choose the "prim and proper" road. And interestingly enough, it happened to be the same road the judges were traveling.

The day after I won the Miss America crown on that glitzy stage, I was whisked off to New York City in a sleek black limousine—the beginning of a year-long schedule filled with travel and appearances. Packed in the trunk were the suitcases I had brought with me to Atlantic City with just enough clothes for one week. What I had with me was hardly a wardrobe suitable for Miss America. At the time, there was no wardrobe prize for the winner, but pageant officials allowed me to take an advance on what I would be making in appearances that year so I could go shopping while I was in New York.

Right after my appearances on the *Good Morning America* and *Today* shows, my chauffeur took me and my traveling companion to several boutiques where the owners had already been notified that we would be coming. The first store specialized in dresses, and the saleswoman had obviously prepared for our arrival. She had pulled out all their most beautiful and most expensive gowns for me to try on. As I looked around, I was quite overwhelmed by the high fashion—and the high price tags! Remember, I had barely finished my sophomore year at BYU, and jeans and sneakers had been my fashion staples. Now, I felt like I was moving to Buckingham Palace. Where to start? None of it seemed real.

I was asked to sit down, and they brought the clothes over to me for my reaction. The first dress was stunning . . . but strapless. It was hard to tell them that it wasn't quite right. The next dress was a glamorous white halter dress . . . with a high slit. I felt like a nerd telling them it wasn't my style. I'm sure they were beginning to wonder, *Well, then, what exactly* is *her style? Cowboy boots?* That would have been closer to the truth.

Finally, I saw a dress that was both stylish and modest. It wasn't my favorite color, but it certainly met my requirements, and it looked good on me. Then, after discarding several other dresses, I saw another, a very glamorous velvet dress that actually kept everything covered, and it was a deep blue color, my favorite. So now, after a discouraging start, I was feeling encouraged that perhaps no matter how immodest trends might be, there would always be something for me to choose from.

Throughout that year, I was introduced to new department stores and boutiques in every city I visited. Since I appeared in approximately five cities a week, that was a lot of shopping! Often, as the salesperson would eagerly try to help me find the perfect outfit, I would encounter the same awkward situation—I would have to somehow make it clear that I wasn't interested in their best-selling, red-hot, low-cut, high-slit, knock-'em-dead, slinky gown. They were always disappointed.

Many times I was asked to be in fashion shows. There it was difficult to control what I would wear because the organizer would already have assigned a list of clothing to each model— even before I arrived in town to offer my opinion. More often than not, however, I would be asked to wear conservative clothing. On the occasions when I wasn't, I would simply ask the person in charge if I could switch with another model. They would usually respond by pointing out that the clothing I had been assigned to wear was actually the priciest, the best-looking, and the most popular. So why didn't I like it? I found the quickest way to get them to comply was to get right to the point and simply say that as much as I liked the outfit, it was a bit immodest for my style. No doubt some of those folks considered me a prude, a goody-goody. But whenever I would get to feeling a bit "not with it," I would think about what the antithesis of a goody-goody might be, and immediately I would feel better about my decisions.

Two or three months into that year, I was introduced to an evening gown designer who had made quite a few of the gowns that had been worn in the Miss America competition that year. His name was Stephen Yearich, and without a doubt, he was the best. He was based in South Carolina, and women actually flew in from all over the country so he could see them in person, take their measurements, discuss their style, and then design a completely original masterpiece. He was, needless to say, expensive; but his uncanny sense for individual style and his expert eye for just the right lines to flatter any figure made his price worth every penny for people in the limelight.

The first time I met him, we immediately hit it off as we joked together about some of the idiosyncrasies of the world of glamour into which we each had fallen. Finally, we began discussing what I expected from his designs and the image I wanted to portray. By then I was well-practiced in saying that anything designed for me was to be "not too high" at the hemline, "not too low" at the neckline.

Stephen gave me a quizzical look and asked, "Are you sure?

It's difficult to design something glamorous unless it is at least a little bit intriguing."

I told him I was sure, and he simply said, "Okay. Then that's the way I'll do it." He probably enjoyed the challenge!

He called me back that afternoon to say he had selected some things for me to look at. He had kept his word, and the wardrobe he showed me *was* modest. In fact, perhaps a bit *too* modest, if there is such a thing! All four outfits covered me from my neck, to my wrist, and to my knee or ankle. One featured so much material wrapped around my neck that I wasn't sure I'd be able to breathe for very long. But the great thing was that all the outfits were modest—*and* quite glamorous. I wore most of them throughout the year and all over the country. I received compliments each time I wore them, and I never, *never* had anybody ask me why I hadn't chosen something a little more revealing.

What I discovered was that people don't notice if a woman is wearing something modest—only if she is wearing something *immodest*. Then it attracts attention to all the wrong things. I happen to like something in turquoise the best, because it draws attention to where I want it—my eyes.

Near the end of my reign, the pageant office in Atlantic City began making preparations for the next Miss America telecast in September. They asked Stephen Yearich to design and coordinate the gowns for myself, another performer, and the mistress of ceremonies, Kathie Lee Gifford.

We all went to Stephen's suite, where he and several assistants were waiting to show us the dresses. Stephen said he had a surprise for me. "I brought my favorite dress that I would like you to wear. It's simple, but it is gorgeous, and you would look fabulous in it!"

He then pulled out a hand-beaded, brilliant red evening gown. It was absolutely stunning, and almost any woman would have given her right arm to wear it. But . . . well, it had "spaghetti" straps and a slit clear up to the thigh. My face didn't light up like Stephen had hoped.

In front of everyone, he questioned, "You don't like it?"

"I *do* like it," I hesitated. "But it's not for me. Maybe I'm a bit strange that way, but I had hoped you would remember my guidelines."

He smiled and then said, "I do remember them. I just thought by now you might have changed. Oh, well. Will you at least try it on, so I can see how it would have looked on you?"

Everyone in the room started begging me to just try it on, and I did. After I put it on, it was even harder to convince the others *and* myself that it just wasn't me. I did like the dress a lot. It was very glamorous. But I reminded myself that it didn't convey the image I wanted to project.

When I told Stephen I needed something more conservative, he smiled and said, "Don't worry. I've already designed the four gowns you will be wearing, and I believe they will each pass your test."

He was right. All four glittering gowns were indeed modest, and they were so beautiful no one would ever have guessed they were designed to be "prim and proper."

Two years later I was married in the Salt Lake Temple, and consequently, any evening gowns I wear in performing or emceeing need to meet "temple standards." Now it's easier than ever to know what I should or shouldn't wear!

I was once approached by a woman who had been very involved in various "Mrs." pageants. Over the years, she had participated in a number of those competitions. She candidly asked how I felt about evening gowns and temple garments. I assumed that she held the opinion (as many women do) that the evening gown worn in competition is a "costume" and that the garment might properly be removed to accommodate the wearing of an immodest dress. Well, I don't buy that. Without hesitation I responded, "I wear both." I hope I didn't offend her, but I never want anyone to wonder exactly where I stand. Have you ever sat on a fence? It's simply not a comfortable place to sit.

I have a good friend whom I respect and admire a great deal, Gretchen Polhemus Jensen. She is a convert to the Church, and to her, the idea of compromising her new beliefs is not even an option.

Gretchen is a very tall, dark-haired beauty from Texas who was Miss USA 1989. At one time she was a horse trainer and a cattle broker. Because of her background in the horse and cattle industry, a company that makes western jeans asked her to model their clothing. Not too long after Gretchen had been married in the temple, she and a few other models were in a dressing room changing into their western wear for a photo shoot. One of the models noticed Gretchen's "different" under-garments, and in an interesting twist, assumed they were the new "in" thing to wear. She asked Gretchen where she could buy some for herself. No doubt with a half-smile, Gretchen simply replied, "You can't buy these, you have to earn them."

Sometimes people are more curious than critical, and while I believe that humor eases a tense situation better than anything else, sometimes a little more explanation is warranted. I like what my dad often says to those who sincerely want to know why we wear temple garments. He tells them that in many churches the leaders wear ornamental robes that symbolize their commitment to their faith. We wear our "symbol of commitment" underneath our clothing, Dad explains, as a reminder to no one but ourselves.

In the professional workplace, where I spend much of my time, the clothes you choose to wear and the image they project are very important. Fortunately, the professional look is also generally a conservative look. Besides, these days, fashion designers recognize that many people insist on having freedom of choice in clothing and that they resist being dictated to about what they will wear.

As a television sportscaster, I have opted to wear pants when I work, simply because of the nature of my job. When I'm sloshing around on a muddy football field in midwinter, I feel pants are more appropriate than a skirt. Any disagreement? But when I occasionally need to wear a skirt on the set, a good measure for me is to make sure my hemline is no higher than the top of my kneecap. I feel comfortable knowing I am not drawing attention to anything other than my face and what I am saying.

I sometimes think about what Alma said to his son Corianton, who, through his immoral behavior, had hindered his father's missionary efforts. Alma reproved his rebellious son by saying, "Behold, O my son, how great iniquity ye brought upon the Zoramites; for when they saw your conduct they would not believe in my words" (Alma 39:11). Think how sad it would be if something in the way we behave created a bad impression of the Church and gave a potential member some reason to turn away, or gave them a false impression of Latter-day Saints.

The way we dress is just one example of our conduct, but we must be willing to dress differently if the popular style is immodest; otherwise, we cannot be the example we should be. How and what we choose to wear *always* sends a signal—whether the recipient of that signal is a cute boy at school or the boss at work, what should that signal say about you? If we women and young women want to be taken seriously and be respected for our skills, we need to wear clothing that says, "I respect my body."

Modesty is about more than the style of clothes we choose to wear. It starts with a core belief that we are literal heirs of God, and as such, we must portray dignity, self-assurance, and determination to preserve all that is sacred. Yes, clothing can say all that about us.

CHAPTER 5

CHOOSING THE WORD OF WISDOM

I was born in Paraguay during the time my dad was working there for Citibank, and for the first four years of my life, our family also lived in the exotic countries of Argentina and Ecuador. While we were in Ecuador, Dad was called to be a mission president, and we lived for the next three years in Mexico. I was too young at the time to understand just how fascinating these places were. But growing up there exposed me to the cultures of those countries, and I learned to speak Spanish.

As I mentioned earlier, when my parents finished their mission assignment, Dad went to work for the Church. Our family moved to Salt Lake City, where he became the head of the Church Purchasing Department.

Living in the heart of "Mormondom" wasn't an entirely comfortable experience for me. For one thing, I wasn't what you would call popular. I felt odd, socially awkward, and definitely not "with it." Looking back, I can see some of the reasons why I felt so out of place: it was hard trying to break into the circles of established friendships and cliques, my clothes were not quite right, and, having grown up in South America, I had a slightly different outlook on life. To make things worse, unlike so many of the girls my age, I didn't like to play with dolls (a football was far more fun), I wasn't into wearing makeup, and in our family we had rules about no Sunday recreation. In fact, even though we were living in the "heart of Zion," our family had lots of rules that some of our Mormon friends and acquaintances didn't seem to follow, and I often wondered why.

When Dad was called as a General Authority five years after moving to Salt Lake, his first assignment was to serve as the Area Supervisor (the title used at that time) for the southern cone of South America: Chile, Argentina, Paraguay, and Uruguay. That meant moving back to a place I only vaguely remembered and relearning a language that had been all but forgotten. But I was thrilled at the news. For me, it was a chance to start all over again. I was glad to be headed back to South America. It never occurred to me that down there I would be considered stranger than ever.

My first week at the American High School in Buenos Aires, Argentina, went okay . . . I guess. I still felt like a stranger, a bit awkward and shy. There were many students of different nationalities attending this small school—French, German, Israeli, Japanese, Swedish, Canadian, Saudi Arabian, and a few other Americans, many of whom were Southern Baptists. By virtue of my nationality and religion, I felt a bit like an outsider. I soon discovered, however, that most of the thirty-five kids in the eighth grade were just like me; none of us had lived very long in Buenos Aires, and we were all struggling to make the adjustment. In other words, I was not the only shy thirteen-year-old who felt lonely and left out.

My English teacher suggested I might enjoy being on the eighth-grade student council. That was a group that would plan activities such as dances, operate the snack bar, and organize fund-raisers for field trips. There were six spots on the council. Six of us raised our hands to be on it, so all six were voted in by the rest of the class. It was the first time I had "won" anything, even if the election was just a formality, and it felt good to be part of a team.

We held our first council meeting that same afternoon. We decided to plan a party for the entire junior high (consisting of about sixty students). We went over every detail, and when we got to the kind of drinks that would be served, someone suggested Coke, and the others all agreed. To them it obviously was no big deal, but I wasn't sure what I should do.

I had been raised to believe that I shouldn't drink cola drinks because of their caffeine content, and caffeine-free Coke was not yet an option. There were only two other members of the Church in our junior high, including my sister Elayne. I wasn't sure if bringing up the subject of serving Coke was worth creating a stir. But I decided to be a little bold.

Just as everyone was ready to move on to the next item on the agenda, I hesitantly asked, "Do we have to have just Coke? I mean, couldn't we order a few bottles of orange Fanta for variety?"

The class president glanced around the council, they all nodded, and she said, "Sure, why not? We'll get a few bottles of Fanta."

I couldn't believe how easy it had been to take a stand. Of course, to them, it wasn't a stand at all, just a suggestion they happened to like. And that suggestion turned out to be the hit of the party . . . at least from my perspective! We had four cases of Coke and one case of Fanta, but the case of Fanta was emptied before any of the others. From then on, at least while I was at the school until my junior year, students were offered a choice. It was hardly anything to boast about, but inside I felt good, and when other kids chose noncola drinks, I felt maybe I wasn't so weird after all. It was a small breakthrough that helped me realize that my opinions, my standards, were just as important as the next guy's. That time it was just a bottle of Coca-Cola; the next time it might be something less trivial. But at least for then, I knew it really wasn't that hard to "just say no."

Gradually, my peers caught on that I didn't necessarily have a yen for orange Fanta, but rather that my family had a specific set of standards by which we were trying to live. Most of the kids thought parts of our Mormon code were amusing if not downright peculiar. Drinking Coke seemed to them to be a harmless thing, and they thought it unnecessarily strict to not date until age sixteen.

I recall one time when a boy in my class came up to me during recess and asked if I wanted to "go with him." I didn't know that to "go with" someone meant to "go steady"—since dating wasn't on my list of things to be familiar with at age thirteen. So I naively asked him, "Go where?" Needless to say, I wasn't asked to go anywhere by a boy for a very long time after that.

I was sometimes teased by my new friends, but I don't remember being criticized or ridiculed. I've often wondered if that wasn't due to the religious diversity of the small international student body. We covered the gamut, from Muslims to Southern Baptists, Buddhists to Jews, Catholics to Mormons. Everyone, it seemed, had something peculiar in their religion. As a result, I became more and more sure of myself and more comfortable standing up for my convictions.

Our class often held parties in private homes, and as I got older and entered my high school years, I found there was more to worry about than just cola drinks. In most of the homes of my classmates, alcoholic beverages were served—especially, of course, at festive occasions like class parties. Fortunately, however, by this time there were several other Mormons at our school, and out of respect for our beliefs, our friends always put out a couple of bottles of Fanta or 7-Up "just for the Mormons." And when we gathered for parties, we Latter-day Saint students would always be warned if the punch had been spiked. In fact, if anyone unknowingly offered one of the Mormons any alcohol or anything containing caffeine, our friends were the first to tell them no! It was understood that if and when the drinking of alcohol began, it was our signal to leave. We accepted any teasing in the spirit it was given—in friendly jest.

One of my classmates in those years wrote in my yearbook that even though she enjoyed teasing me, she respected me because I lived by a code. She also wrote that she wished she had the strength of character to declare a belief and then live by it.

In the years since then, I have found that most people I deal with feel the same way. They may not agree with the way I try to live, but they generally respect my right to be different. For my part, I have never felt the need to apologize for my standards or to hide my convictions. You'll probably find, as I have, that if you don't make a big deal of it or give the impression that you're disgusted by those who drink or smoke, it is usually an acceptable thing to just say "No, thank you" when you're offered cigarettes, alcohol, and so on. Only rarely do you run into anyone who wants to quarrel with a courteous refusal. Many people are health-conscious these days, and it is not uncommon to find a person who recognizes the harmful effects of tobacco and alcohol, aside from any religious consideration. If someone does take issue with your refusal, I have found that a sense of humor sometimes helps. And if they press you to know why you don't use alcohol or tobacco, that often provides an opportunity to explain the gospel.

While living in South America, my mom and dad encountered some potentially awkward social situations, which they were always able to defuse. On one occasion Dad was the host at an important meeting of top bankers from some twenty Latin American nations, held in Asunción, Paraguay. One of his duties was to serve as master of ceremonies at a formal dinner—a dinner at which the president of the nation himself would be in attendance. Protocol required that Dad propose a toast to the president and to the country, and he was worried about how to do this without using the traditional champagne.

At that time only a few cities in Latin America had culinary water systems that were safe enough to drink from. But Dad's bank had helped fund a recently constructed system for the capital city. At the dinner, there were the usual four glasses in front of everyone's plate. One was for red wine, one for white wine, one for champagne, and one for sparkling water. Dad had turned three of his four long-stemmed glasses upside down and had asked the head waiter to bring him a large pitcher of water straight from the tap.

When the moment came for him to propose the toast, he spoke into the microphone to get everyone's attention and then, with something of a flourish, poured clear water from the pitcher into his glass. Setting the pitcher down and raising his glass toward the dinner guests, he smiled broadly and announced, "I don't know what you have in your glasses, but in mine I have the purest of liquids: drinking water from the municipal water system of our capital city—Asunción, Paraguay!"

Dad recalls: "With that statement there was first laughter and then applause. I continued, 'And with my raised glass I invite you to join me in a toast to our host country, the great Republic of Paraguay, and to [its] president who honors us with his presence.' I drank my tap water to his and the country's honor and then continued with similar toasts to several other dignitaries. No one ever forgot my 'Mormon toast'!"

On another occasion, this time in Argentina, Mom and Dad were invited to a magnificent country estate. After a tour of the mansion they were led into an impressive dining room. There, using a lavish three-hundred-year-old China and silver service, their British hosts had prepared a formal "high tea" service for a sizable group of people.

Mom and Dad were aware that tea in the British setting can be either a normal tea with crackers or cookies, or "high tea," which is a formal event where a certain protocol is observed.

Mom and the wife of another guest were asked to assist the hostess, who sat between them and presided at the ceremony. Mom was to assist by passing the cups and saucers to the hostess, who would pour hot water into them and hand them to her second assistant hostess. She would then ask the person to be served, "One tea bag or two?" and each person would specify what he or she wished. She would follow up by inquiring, "One lump of sugar or two?"

My parents were caught in a social dilemma. They were representing the largest bank in the world and were being given the best red-carpet treatment. How should they handle the situation without compromising their standards or offending their hosts?

Dad later wrote: "All this was done with gracious perfection, smiles, and small talk appropriate to the occasion. When I could see that it was my cup coming next, I quietly asked, 'May I have a slice of lemon only in the water, please?' A perfect hostess in the midst of a flawless high tea protocol is not going to cause a scene. She answered, 'Certainly,' and passed the plate of lemon slices to my wife and said, 'Your husband would like a slice of lemon in his tea cup.' Helen followed instructions, preparing the same 'lemon tea' for herself when it was her turn to be served. The hostess poured the hot water into the cup and passed it to her second assistant, who asked, 'Would you like a tea bag?' to which I responded, 'No, thank you, only the lemon. But I will take one cube of sugar.' We were each given what we had requested," my dad wrote, "and no one made any remarks or seemed to take note of it."

I have found that if one is hesitant or apologetic, it creates socially awkward situations, and it sometimes reflects poorly on the Church. In fact, hesitation can be mistaken for doubt or weakness. If we do not convey with certainty that we are settled in our convictions, we become vulnerable to ridicule or taunting. There are plenty of people out there who may know little else about the Church but who have heard about our Word of Wisdom. If someone is known to be a Mormon, and he or she doesn't take a stand, it can be like spilling blood in shark-infested waters. Even if you are not attacked, you can be sure there is little or no respect afforded a "waffler" who can't decide which way to go.

On a recent trip to Israel, my husband, Bob, and I had the good fortune to meet Paul and Maureen Clayton, an LDS couple who had previously lived in Germany for a number of years and currently live in Israel. Paul works for the United States government, and in his information-sensitive job, he often worked with German police organizations. His official duties frequently required him to attend social functions where alcohol was served. He told us, "The Germans are very proud of their beer. To them, it is more than a mere beverage; it is a treasured part of their culture, and some of them raise their babies on it!" Paul said that every year he is required to attend a certain huge beer bash and barbecue. For the first two years, he politely refused the beer that was offered him, and though his hosts were incredulous, they provided soft drinks as a substitute. Because the Germans take their beer very seriously, he knew he had to be diplomatic, but he also made it clear that it was part of his religion to abstain from drinking alcohol.

After a couple of years of this, the gentleman who presided over the annual party finally got the message and Paul never had to refuse again. In fact, out of respect for Paul, the host not only personally served Paul a soft drink, but once, he also put his arm around Paul's shoulders and announced to everyone at the party, "This is my good Mormon friend, and he is to be served only juice and sodas." Paul's wife, Maureen, wrote us a letter telling of the experience: "Paul managed to handle a potentially tricky situation with tact and without compromising his standards. The result has been that he has gained the respect and trust of the German officials. Paul is known as a man who sticks to his principles despite social pressure—even professional social pressure—to do otherwise. In the long run, the respect of others is earned by not being afraid to stand alone in a crowd."

Paul had developed the courage of his convictions through faith and experience. Where can the young men and women of the Church find that same courage? For many teenagers, standing "alone in a crowd" can be a difficult thing to do, especially since most are still forming their opinions on just about everything and intently working on shaping and building their self-image. Worrying about what other people think is a time-consuming part of most teenagers' lives. But with a little faith, a little desire to stand for something, and the knowledge of right and wrong, it really isn't hard at all to make a decision before the situation arises.

When my husband, Bob, was twelve years old, he was invited to take part in a cattle roundup on his sister-in-law's 40,000-acre ranch in Wyoming. This was no "dude" ranch, nor was the roundup simply contrived as a form of entertainment. This would be hard, dusty, and downright dirty work. And Bob could hardly wait! When he arrived for this weekend rendezvous with roughly two thousand head of cattle, he immediately searched out the ranch hands who, in his mind, held the ultimate summer job—doing nothing but ropin' calves and ridin' the range. They were as close as he was going to get to the heroes of the Wild West—both fictional and real—that he had always admired. On that first day, Bob struck up a friendship with a young eighteen-year-old cowhand who seemed to fit the tough images in Bob's mind. This young man could handle a horse and rope with coolness. And as if Bob needed additional reason to be impressed, the cowhand gave him a token of their friendship—a rattle from a rattlesnake he had recently killed on the trail. Needless to say, Bob was eager to be liked and accepted by this tough guy.

The spring roundup was about to begin, and as Bob stood next to his saddled mount waiting with all the ranch hands for the word to move out, his new friend came over, casually leading his horse by the reins. He stopped, bent over, yanked up his pant leg, then pulled a small pouch out of his boot. Turning to Bob, he asked him if he wanted some chewing tobacco for the ride.

Now I would guess that many young men (or even young women) might hesitate in this situation, even if they plan on giving the right answer. After all, this was a gesture of acceptance, coming from someone he admired. It's not easy to risk offending someone you look up to. But one of the first traits I discovered and admired in Bob when we began dating was that he never determines his course of action based on what others might think. Bob's philosophy even as a young boy has always been uncomplicated: There can be no hesitation when it is a matter of right or wrong.

Bob's quick and solid reply neither offended the young man nor left room for argument: "No, thanks, I don't chew," he said.

The ranch hand responded as he put a wad of tobacco under his lip, "Yeah, it's a bad habit. I've got to quit sometime." That was it. The roundup began, and Bob had the time of his life!

This approach is certainly not new; we've all heard of the "Just Say No to Drugs" campaign. Yet it really is that simple. It's a matter of deciding beforehand. In today's world, no matter what the religious influence, there is a general consensus that drug abuse cannot be tolerated in our society. Even so, many are tempted by drugs.

One area I'm especially familiar with is the sports world where athletes are driven by the ever-increasing need to compete and to continually better themselves. Though today there are strict regulations in place concerning the use of performance-enhancing drugs, somehow these drugs still slip through the cracks—available to most athletes, from the beginner all the way to the world-class professional. I have several friends who have reached the top of their discipline, yet from their earliest years have made the decision that drugs would simply not be an option to help them achieve their goals.

One of those friends, four-time Olympian Henry Marsh, told me about the time at a major international event when he saw one of his competitors take some pills. Henry suspected they were masking agents for steroids, and later, when it was revealed that this team had in fact been regularly taking steroids, his suspicions were confirmed. But just before that particular race, Henry, still thinking of his desire to be number one in the world, had nevertheless renewed his commitment to do the best he could with his *natural* abilities, disciplined training, and the Lord's help—and nothing else. He subsequently held the number one spot in the world for three years.

When I was almost seventeen and in the second semester of my junior year of high school, we moved back to Salt Lake City. I was by then older and more confident, not quite as shy, and I knew what I stood for. But living in and going to school in Salt Lake was different than I expected. I was surprised to discover Mormon kids dating before they were sixteen and wearing strapless dresses to proms. I had been used to abiding by black-and-white standards in South America, and now I was faced with a confusing "gray" set of rules. Among my new acquaintances I saw different levels of commitment to the standards of the Church, and I found that for me it had actually been easier to live the gospel in Argentina.

Then, in September 1984, I once again found myself in a position I much preferred—being "different" and in the minority. In the spotlight, there is no gray. It's all very black and white. You either say exactly who you are, then make sure your actions are consistent with your claims, or you don't take a stand at all. I chose to say exactly who I was and what I believed in, knowing I was creating unusually high expectations that I would always be held accountable for.

As Dad described earlier, my initial audience for this scrutiny of my beliefs was the cynical and probing press corps that covered the Miss America competition in Atlantic City. But that was only the beginning of that kind of examination of my beliefs.

The day after the pageant ended, I was escorted by one of my two assigned traveling companions, by limousine, to the upscale Intercontinental Hotel in downtown Manhattan, New York. As we entered our suite, I took in the glamorous and ritzy surroundings—the living room, the dining room, the Jacuzzi—and then noticed a huge basket of goodies. To the side of it was a large bottle of champagne. Now, I have no idea what the difference is between a good and a bad bottle of champagne, but this one sure *looked* expensive. It was covered with black and gold foil. I casually mentioned to my companion how good the fruit in the basket looked, but that it would have been nice to have some apple juice or something.

With a quizzical look on her face, she turned to me and, holding up the bottle, asked, "You mean, you don't want this?" When I told her that I don't drink, she said, "Oh, that's right. Now I remember what you said in your press conference. Do you mind if I have some?"

I said that was fine, to which she replied, "I'm sure going to enjoy traveling with you!"

I found out then what I was to rediscover during that entire year of endless cocktail parties and high-level corporate dinners: I didn't have to prove anything by the type of drink I held in my hand—a simple Perrier sparkling water with lime was absolutely no big deal. I never experienced anyone looking down their nose at me because I had chosen a nonalcoholic drink. It just never became an issue, although occasionally someone who had had a bit too much to drink would say, "Come on! Loosen up!" I'd just smile at them and move on at the first chance.

When I went to work for ESPN in spring 1988, I encountered a slightly different situation. I was no longer required to attend cocktail parties and fancy dinners. Now my environment was more like a locker room! At ESPN, the "total sports network," our work was centered around the game. Most of the people I worked with were forty or younger, and there was a "team" feeling in our organization.

ESPN is mostly a men's club. Sometimes the men remember to watch their language when women are around, and sometimes they don't—thus the locker-room atmosphere. In an attempt to fit in, some of the few women who work there have adopted the men's penchant for rough language.

Obviously, anyone who works at ESPN simply loves sports, and after a broadcast we sometimes feel as though we've just finished playing ourselves because we are so exhausted. Believe it or not, working behind the scenes in television, especially live television, is an intense and stressful mental workout. Everyone works hard to make sure a completely first-rate program is produced, and when the work is done, our crew is in desperate need of relaxation.

Often we will meet for dinner, and some of the crew will head for a bar first. (Some of my colleagues who have been assigned to cover BYU football games in Provo, Utah, have shared with me their woes in not being able to find a suitable place there to wind down after a game!) When I have my own car, it's very simple for me to say that I'm tired and would rather go back to the hotel or to arrange to meet them later for dinner. But when I don't have a car, I'm dependent on the others for transportation. Fortunately, I haven't been seriously trapped. In those situations when the others are deciding between a bar and a restaurant, I have been able to convince them that we are all more hungry than thirsty, so why not head directly to the restaurant?

In December 1987, I was given my first assignment with ESPN. I was to work as a sideline reporter at the Holiday Bowl in San Diego. Since I had worked at two previous Holiday Bowls for KSL-TV in Salt Lake, I should have been comfortable in the role. But I was a little nervous. I had not yet been hired full time by ESPN, so, in essence, this was my audition. They wanted to see if I could do a professional job, if I could fit in with the staff—basically, they wanted to decide if they liked me. I very much wanted to be liked.

Following the game, I was feeling pretty good about my performance, and the producer complimented me on my work. He said that he felt I had a future with ESPN. Naturally, I was excited to think that perhaps I was fitting in. I had ridden to Jack Murphy Stadium with one of the associate producers, and now everyone was talking about having a drink and going to dinner. I was truly exhausted and just wanted to go back to the hotel and give my husband a call. But I couldn't. Not when I was close to making "the team," not when I needed to make a good impression. Besides, I wasn't driving.

I had been to San Diego many times before, and I remembered a great Mexican restaurant in Old Town, located in a historic district of the city. I suggested that if we went there directly, we probably wouldn't have to wait too long to get in. Everyone agreed. I had successfully avoided going to the bar.

We got to the restaurant pretty quickly and were seated outside in the garden while waiting for a table. Naturally, I was anxious to be accepted by the other seven people in our party—all about the same age as I was, all professionals.

When a waitress asked if she could bring us something to drink while waiting for dinner, it occurred to me that I was in somewhat of an awkward situation. If I ordered something nonalcoholic, there was a chance they would think I was peculiar. By the time it was my turn to order, though, I had realized that my thoughts were letting me down, and I refused to be intimidated. Besides, they wouldn't really care what I ordered, would they?

I told the waitress, "I'd like a virgin [nonalcoholic] straw-berry daiquiri, please."

"Did you say virgin strawberry daiquiri?"

"Yes, please."

Well, at this point, all seven pairs of ears were pointed at me, not sure they had heard correctly, either. Okay, that made me feel a bit stupid, but I wasn't about to let them see through me. If you're apologetic, you become easy prey.

One guy joked, "Can't handle the strong stuff, huh?"

I laughed, then pleasantly replied, "Actually, I wouldn't know. I've never tried the 'strong stuff,' since I don't drink."

That became the topic of conversation for the next few minutes until the waitress brought our drinks. I took one sip of mine and about choked. It was definitely not nonalcoholic. The producer, who was sitting next to me, took a sip of mine and said no, it was just fine, there was no alcohol in it. I hated to make a scene, but I knew there was something alcoholic in it, so I called the waitress back and told her there was alcohol in my drink. She looked at me as if to say, "So? Lighten up—what harm will a little alcohol do?" I got her to try it. She nodded her head and said she would get me a new drink. My new friends teased me the rest of the night, but I could tell it was because they liked me, not because they disapproved of me.

ESPN hired me, and a couple of months later, before the contract had been finalized, I was given another assignment by the network. This time I went to Aspen, Colorado, as a feature reporter, to cover the U.S. alpine skiing championships.

I was told that ESPN had hired two U.S. team skiers (who had been injured and were out of the competition) to be the color analysts for our live coverage. One of them was downhill skier Pam Fletcher, whom I had wanted to meet for a long time. Even after she was injured in a freak accident at the Calgary Olympics, which destroyed her chances for a medal, she remained positive and became a strong, ardent supporter of the rest of the team at the 1988 Olympic finish line. She was well known as an enthusiastic, cheerful person, and I was looking forward to working with her and getting to know her better.

On my first afternoon in Aspen, I decided to go to the ESPN compound and take a look at the facilities. While I was wandering around, I ran into Pam and introduced myself, not sure if she would even care who I was. But to my surprise, she was even more approachable than I had hoped, and after talking for just a few minutes, we had become friends. She asked me if I would like to join her and a few of her buddies for dinner that night. I tried not to act too excited. Here I had just met a world-class athlete I had been dying to meet, and she was inviting me into her circle of friends! As calmly as I could, I asked where I should meet her.

She said, "Why don't we go get a drink first? There's a great bar just down the street from the hotel. We can have a drink and then meet up with the group."

As you might imagine, I didn't want to give her any reason to think I might not be fun to hang around with. And I certainly didn't want to give her any reason to think I was odd. *That might kill a friendship before it even got started,* I thought. So I gave a lame excuse rather than the real reason.

"I don't think I'll be able to make it before dinner," I said. "I've got some things I have to finish up with ESPN first, and I haven't unpacked yet. Why don't you go on ahead, and I'll catch up with you?" We agreed to meet in the hotel lobby at 6:30, and from there we would go to dinner.

When I got to the lobby, Pam was just making her way down a flight of stairs. It took her awhile because of her broken leg. With a big smile on her face, she said that everyone was running late. We had a half hour to kill, so why not go have a drink? There it was again.

As she turned to hobble toward the door, I figured I'd better explain the cold, hard facts.

"Pam," I said.

"Yes?"

"Pam, I don't drink . . . I hope you don't mind if I don't go out with you to get a drink."

She looked at me for a second and then said, "That's so cool!"

I couldn't believe my ears! "It is?"

"Yeah. I've been meaning to cut it out completely, but it's so easy to get in the habit. You know, I'd like to stop altogether. Why don't we just wait in the hotel lounge area and get a club soda or something?"

It was so easy. I just wanted to kick myself for being even the slightest bit embarrassed about my no-alcohol standard. But on the other hand, maybe it was better that I had been somewhat reticent about advertising it to the world. There's nothing that turns people off quite so quickly as a pompous, self-righteous person with a holier-than-thou attitude. We need to be assertive without being obnoxious.

The funny part about all this is that there are more and more people like Pam, who, because it's the healthy thing to do, are trying to "cut it out altogether." These days, those who choose to abstain from alcohol are often viewed as being smart and are admired for the self-control they are able to exercise. Among informed people, the days of ridiculing teetotalers as "dweebs" or "nerds" seem to be gone, at least among adult professionals. But, even so, being seen as odd is really not all that bad. Take advantage of the fact that you stand out, that you are different, that you are noticed. Work harder and more efficiently than anyone else, and then you will be admired—both for your strengths and for your peculiarities.

Far from being a detriment to me socially or to my career, living the Word of Wisdom has been a positive thing. Explaining why I don't drink or smoke has often been an effective icebreaker when meeting new people, and it has given me many opportunities to explain other aspects of the Church. As far as I'm concerned, there is no need to ever apologize for living any of the principles of the gospel, and if you treat the questions that come up honestly and with good humor, the chance of offending somebody is just about zero. In fact, chances are they will be impressed by the health code you live.

CHAPTER 6

KEEPING THE SABBATH DAY HOLY

There was a time in my life when I didn't exactly look forward to Sunday. I was young, and I didn't particularly need to "rest," so naturally, I often felt frustrated on that day because of the many things I couldn't do. And I could never figure out why the best day of the week—the sunniest day of the week—always seemed to fall on Sunday. I decided it had to be Satan's way of trying to tempt us.

I had faith in my parents' strict rules for Sunday behavior, but that didn't keep me from wondering why I was allowed to sit by the swimming pool in my dress and read the scriptures but couldn't get into the water. By the time I was fifteen or sixteen, I was beginning to understand a little bit more, but I have to admit, I still didn't like feeling so restricted. And since I spent most of my young life living among people who viewed Sunday as the best play day of the week, I was constantly reminded of how "deprived" I was by having to explain to my friends the things I was not allowed to do. It was just one more piece of evidence to them that we Mormons really were different.

In Buenos Aires, Argentina, the summers aren't just hot, they are blistering. They aren't just muggy, they are steamy. And in the middle-class neighborhood where we lived, having a swimming pool in the backyard was about as common as owning a TV. Even if the backyard was barely big enough for a couple of lawn chairs and a barbecue, somehow a pool would be squeezed in.

My bedroom was on the third floor of our house, and it overlooked all the backyards on our block. So on a hot Sunday afternoon, when I would be trying to concentrate on writing letters, reading, and writing in my journal, I could hear all the splashing and the squealing voices of happy children playing and cooling off in their swimming pools. If I wanted to escape the heat and the distractions, I would have to retreat to either the living room or my parents' room, the only rooms in the house that were air-conditioned.

Yes, at times I was irritated that *everyone* didn't see the Sabbath as a special day. It would have made it much easier for me to obey the rules and enjoy the day for what it is supposed to be. But as I look back, I can appreciate what Mom and Dad were trying to teach us—that Sunday is not a day for recreation or work. Rather, it's a day set aside for us to worship the Lord, nourish our spirits, evaluate ourselves, and gather strength for the coming week. It is a sacred day, not just for the Lord but also for us.

As I mentioned earlier, my parents were often in sticky situations during my dad's banking career in South America. They were often invited to be the houseguests of business or government officials, and sometimes that involved staying in someone's home on a Sunday.

Dad dealt with these situations by being totally open with his hosts, explaining to them why he was committed to observing the Sabbath and what kinds of activities he wished to avoid. He and Mom found that people were generally understanding and considerate, even interested in the reasons behind their religious observances.

My younger sister, Elayne, and I discovered that not everyone was that tolerant of our beliefs about Sunday activities. We both enjoyed participating in sports while we attended the American High School in Buenos Aires, and since our high school consisted of only about one hundred fifty students, we had ample opportunity to be on just about any team we wanted. Elayne and I competed in volleyball, track, softball, soccer, and swimming. We were busy and we loved it.

Our friends at the school were quite diverse in their beliefs, but none of them seemed to have the same problem that we Mormons did regarding athletic competition on Sundays. That became an issue during my sophomore year, prior to the last and biggest swim meet of the season.

About fifteen of the best teams in the province of Buenos Aires had gathered at a downtown indoor swimming pool for what was the equivalent of a state meet. It was so sauna-like in the building that I wondered if it wouldn't have been better to be outside in the direct South American sun. It was a Saturday morning, and we were competing for a chance to be in the finals, which were to be held the next day. I didn't expect to do well enough to qualify, so I never gave a thought to what I would do if I won.

I was fifteen years old and well into my second year of high school competition. I thought the butterflies in my stomach would have become weary from their ceaseless flapping, but such was not the case. My legs turned into noodles, and my arms seemed disconnected from my body, but somehow I pushed off the block when the gunshot signaled the start of our heat in the 4 x 100–meter free-style relay. Elayne was a member of my team, and when I touched the wall with a slight lead, she shot off the block and kept up the pace. Our team won the race, and suddenly we were in the finals. The finals! That meant our team would be racing on Sunday. But before I could explain our dilemma to the coach, I had another heat to swim, the individual 100-meter backstroke. I figured my coach could wait a few minutes to hear the bad news.

Coming off an exciting win in the relay, I was feeling more relaxed and energetic than I expected. The gun went off, and I began churning as fast as I knew how. I hardly peeked at my competition, but when I did, right after the turn, I found I was in front! The adrenaline kicked in and I made myself go a bit faster. I didn't even feel tired until I touched the wall. As I struggled to catch my breath, I was hugged by my teammates and my coach, and then I realized—I had qualified for the finals on Sunday.

On our team, the times from our relay and my individual backstroke were the only ones good enough to make the finals. But for as long as I could remember, I had been taught that Sunday was unique. It was sacred, and it was not a day for activities that could be performed on other days of the week. Elayne and I went to our coach and explained the situation and respectfully asked for permission to withdraw from the finals on Sunday.

She didn't take it well. In fact, she exploded and accused us of being quitters and poor sports because we were letting the team down. In all fairness to her, we should have informed her before the meet started that we would be unable to participate on Sunday. But, as I have indicated, I really didn't think it would become an issue, since I didn't think I would make it into the finals.

Well, now it *was* an issue. Soon our teammates got wind of our predicament, and they came after us, too. They felt we were letting the team down, and to be quite honest, I began to feel that way also. But the more they backed us up against the wall, the more we defended our position, until they finally left in disgust. All but the coach. She still had something to say.

A similar situation had developed a few months earlier. During a huge, three-day track meet—billed as the largest high school track meet in the world, with close to twenty thousand participants from all over Argentina—I had qualified for the finals in the 100-meter hurdles but had chosen not to compete because the finals were on Sunday. My swim coach was also the track coach, and this was the last straw.

She said she had had it with our peculiarities, and because of this latest stunt, I was no longer a member of the swim team. *And,* she added, since I wouldn't be needing them any longer, I could also turn in my softball and volleyball uniforms. She happened to also be the softball and volleyball coach!

I was angry and hurt. How could she do that to me just for sticking to a personal belief? But after reviewing the situation, I could understand her frustration. She was trying to field the best team possible, and we had pulled the rug out from under her. Even so, it seemed unreasonable for her to throw me off *all* the teams. Fortunately, she eventually reinstated me, and I recall saying a silent prayer, thanking the Lord for another chance after I had carelessly neglected to inform my coach of the rules I play by.

I had learned my lesson. So in another similar incident, I took a different approach. I decided to discuss my standards *before* any crisis arose.

It was a yearly tradition at Lincoln High School in Buenos Aires to participate in a week-long competition against one of the other American high schools from a neighboring country, competing in team sports such as soccer, basketball, volleyball, and softball. Sometimes our teams would travel abroad for a week, and other times, we would host our international opponent.

One year we were invited to Paraguay for the games, and when I saw the itinerary, I knew I would have a problem. We were to arrive on Saturday, and the biggest day of competition would be on Sunday. Only a limited number of athletes would be invited to go, and preference was given to those who could play on more than one team. I knew that if I balked at the schedule, I would be replaced in a heartbeat.

The star of the men's basketball team, Mike Bishop, was the mission president's son, and his brother, Steve, was also a key player on that team. They were both also on the men's softball and volleyball teams. I knew that nothing would be changed if it were just me complaining. But if *all* of us were to ask for a change, maybe the coaches would do something so the three of us could go.

We approached our coaches with our request. My coach just gave me a disgusted look and a sigh that said to me, "I thought we already had enough of this foolish behavior." But since there were three of us, and since we were involved on several of the teams, they were willing to try to figure out a way to modify the schedule. Apparently, it wasn't too difficult, because not long after we spoke to our coaches, we were told we would leave on Monday and be home by Saturday! Based on my previous experience, I hadn't really expected them to be so cooperative. But now they were rearranging an entire international competition (okay, so it was just a couple of high schools getting together from across the border) for the sake of three of us who had said we wouldn't participate on Sunday.

I guess it was a little risky to take the position we did. It's possible we all might have been left at home. But unless we were willing to compromise our standards, we had no choice but to be forthright and honest. It worked for us, and I imagine that, on the high school level at least, unless *all* the games are played on Sunday, most coaches would be willing to accommodate an athlete who is dedicated, hardworking, self-motivated, and enthusiastic, especially if he or she is a talented player.

But what about the athletes who *aren't* the key players on the team? The ones who are expendable, as I would have been if I hadn't had the additional support of the others? The bottom line is simple: Often the choice *has* to be made between one option or the other. Just ask, *What will this decision say about me and about my integrity?*

I absolutely love this headline I read in the *Deseret News* on February 15, 1995: "Herring Chooses Sabbath over NFL." It was a story about Eli Herring, the 6'8", 335-pound offensive tackle who played collegiate football at BYU. Eli had the skill and size to make it in the pro ranks. He was projected to go in the first or second round of the NFL draft, a position that would mean the possibility of a very lucrative contract. He and his wife, Jennifer, had an eleven-month-old baby daughter at the time, and they certainly could have used the money. In addition, Eli loved playing football and had dreamed for most of his life about being in the NFL.

But in the face of all that, Eli Herring announced that he

was not going to enter the draft—not because he wasn't healthy but because of his principles. He told the press that more than wanting to play in the NFL, he wanted to keep the Ten Commandments, specifically the fourth: "Remember the Sabbath Day, to keep it holy." To Herring, that meant no working—or playing football—on Sundays.

"It was a tough decision," he said. "I've thought about playing pro football since I was a kid. But NFL games are on Sunday, and as I was growing up, my family always recognized Sunday as the Sabbath. For me, personally, it just wouldn't be right." Asked what he'd do if a team went ahead and drafted him, Eli said, "It would be a wasted draft pick, because I've made up my mind not to play on Sunday." He was, in fact, drafted high, and the press speculated that he might then change his mind. He didn't.

With literally millions of dollars at stake, Eli Herring acted on his principles and gave up an opportunity that comes to only a few athletes. The sporting world was generally incredulous, but Eli didn't consider what he had done any big deal. I can't tell you how much I admire him for taking that kind of stand. Imagine the legacy he has given his children, and consider the powerful example he has provided the rest of us.

Another classic example of an athlete who was true to his beliefs is gymnast Peter Vidmar, gold medalist at the 1984 Olympics in Los Angeles:

> Peter loved gymnastics and was trained at the Culver City Gymnastics Club by Makato Sakamoto. "Mako" was an Olympian himself, and he had a dream of developing one of his protégés into an Olympic champion. He found Peter a willing pupil, and sensing Peter's potential, Mako gradually

extended their workouts, eventually suggesting they add Sunday to their training schedule.

Peter had just turned 12 and had been ordained a deacon in the Aaronic Priesthood. Much as he loved gymnastics, he couldn't in good conscience put the sport ahead of his priesthood and [ahead] of Sunday.

He told Mako that he couldn't train on Sunday and hoped he would understand. Mako didn't. He responded the way you'd expect a coach to respond: he dismissed Peter from the team. If Mako was willing to give 100 percent to a developing gymnast, a gymnast he believed had world-class potential, and that gymnast wasn't willing to give 100 percent back, then they had a problem.

Mako, suspecting the decision not to practice on Sunday had been made by Peter's parents, visited them soon afterward. John and Doris Vidmar explained that Peter's decision was completely his own, and that it wasn't based on a lack of loyalty to the Culver City Gymnastics Club. To the contrary, his quandary was wondering how he could be loyal to both God and gymnastics if they each wanted him on Sunday.

If anything could sway Mako Sakamoto, it was commitment—any kind of commitment. He saw this as commitment. He asked Peter to rejoin the club. [Peter rejoined the club and repaid Mako for his efforts when he later won the Olympic gold medal] (Lee Benson and Doug Robinson, *Trials and Triumphs: Mormons in the Olympic Games* [Salt Lake City: Deseret Book Company, 1992], pp. 125, 128).

As members of the Church, we are somewhat peculiar in our view of keeping the Sabbath day holy. There are many good, religious people in our society for whom attending a basketball game or going to a movie or to an amusement park does not constitute "breaking the Sabbath." We need to be careful not to condemn them for their views. But sometimes, without causing a lot of waves, we can be instrumental in making a few changes.

When I was hosting an ESPN program called *Scholastic Sports America,* which focuses on high school athletes, I was assigned to do a story in Yakima, Washington, on a heptathlete. While in Yakima, I happened to meet an LDS young woman by the name of Tricia Hartley. She was the daughter of a bishop, and she asked me if I could help her with a decision she had to make.

Tricia told me that she had always wanted to be involved in the Junior Miss program, but there was a problem. The local competition was being held on a Sunday. She asked me what I would do. I told her that she would have to make that decision, but I related the experiences I have described about my high school days in South America and told her how we had succeeded in getting our coaches to actually change the schedule away from Sunday. I asked her if she had inquired whether the date of the contest was set in cement—could it possibly be changed? She replied she hadn't; she was sure that a seventeen-year-old would have no influence on such an important matter. But Tricia told me she would ask if the date could be changed.

Here is an excerpt from a note she sent me not long after:

> I wanted you to know they are going to change the date of the Junior Miss Pageant to Saturday. When I first talked to the director, he was quite rude about the subject. But when he took it to the committee, they all saw various reasons why it would be better to hold it on Saturday.

Tricia showed exemplary courage, and in her case, as in my one instance, things turned out well, and she didn't have to compete on Sunday or forgo the competition altogether. It won't always work that way. There may be times when standing up *will* result in losing our dreams, as happened to Eli Herring. But our actions will be remembered and respected.

Remember Mike Bishop, the mission president's son who was the star of our high school basketball team? When I was a freshman in high school, Mike was a junior, and he had an experience that year in which he stood up for his belief of the Sabbath in a way that changed the course of several lives, and changed them forever.

The varsity high school basketball, volleyball, softball, and soccer teams were preparing to travel to Peru for a four-day competition with the American school in Lima. Mike was on the basketball team, and when he discovered that his team was scheduled to play on Sunday, he immediately went to the school's athletic director, Profe (meaning "Professor"), and asked him to send someone else in his place, someone who would be able to compete on that day. Well, when Mike's basketball coach, Lenny Ascuito, discovered that his star player was planning on staying home from this important competition, he went straight to Profe and insisted they simply change the day of the basketball game. At the time, it struck Lenny as a bit odd for a teenage boy to feel so strongly about something like that, but since his main concern was getting Mike to play, he shrugged it off.

Mike joined his team for the trip to Peru, and after arriving, they were invited by their Peruvian hosts to a party for all the teams—on Sunday. Lenny was one of the chaperones, and he began counting heads at the party. All his players were there but one. He asked the other guys on the team where Mike was.

"He's reading the Bible," they said.

"C'mon. Give me a better excuse," Lenny insisted.

"No, Coach. He's a Mormon—you don't have to worry about him."

Lenny found it difficult to believe that a young man, on a high school trip to a foreign country, away from his parents, would be studying the scriptures instead of attending a party. Still, something told him that's exactly what his star player was doing. He was impressed—and intrigued.

On the flight back to Buenos Aires, a three-hour flight, Lenny asked Mike if he could sit next to him. The coach wanted to find out more about this young man who exhibited total commitment to his religious beliefs.

Of course, Mike cleared the seat for his coach to sit down, and Lenny began asking questions.

"What do you Mormons believe? Do you believe in Christ? I've heard about your Tabernacle Choir, but that's it."

Now you need to know something about Mike: he is the quintessential mission president's son. He attended zone conferences whenever he could, regularly went tracting with the missionaries, knew all the discussions, and carried pamphlets and copies of the Book of Mormon wherever he went. He had learned well from his parents. Little did Lenny know what he was in for.

So, before they landed, Mike had given him the first discussion, invited him to another, and had given Lenny all his pamphlets and a Book of Mormon.

Lenny wasn't sure what to think about all he had heard, but

he was convinced that Mike really believed what he was talking about, and that kept the coach's interest.

Over the next few months, the Bishop family invited Lenny and his fiancée, Adriana, over to their home to hear the missionary discussions and to eat Sister Bishop's famous homemade bread. Lenny was attending medical school at the time, so it was difficult to follow a regular schedule, but the day after Lenny and Adriana got married, the two were baptized. One year later, they were sealed in the Salt Lake Temple, and three years later, Lenny was called to be a bishop. Dr. Ascuito has since served in other callings, including stake high councilor. Today he serves in his ward's bishopric, and Adriana is the Primary president. They have three beautiful children.

Mike's commitment to keeping the Sabbath day holy was the thing that originally attracted Lenny's attention. Mike's example will have joyous eternal consequences for the Ascuito family.

Frequently, *how* to keep the Sabbath day holy is not a clear-cut matter. It is not as simple as determining "Do I run or not run?" Many of us have jobs that require either occasional Sunday travel or occasional work on Sunday. We are not always able to dictate when or where we will work.

At the beginning of the Great Depression, my Grandpa Walser had no choice but to take the only job offered to him— a job working in the carpentry section of the Southern Pacific Railroad in El Paso, Texas. My mom recalls that her father was required to work, not only on Sundays, but *every* day, from 7:00 A.M. to 3:00 P.M. Those were difficult years, yet he was one of the few who had a full-time job, one that allowed him to clothe and feed his family of nine. For thirty years, until he retired,

Grandpa worked seven days a week. He provided for his family the best and only way he knew how. Fortunately, Church meetings were held during the evening back then, and so even though he had to work on Sundays, he never missed going to sacrament meeting.

For some, there might not be a choice. But for others, there are options from which to choose. Sometimes it becomes a matter of priorities. Should I take the job with better pay that requires Sunday work, or should I be content with a job that pays a lesser salary and provides Sunday off? It may boil down to this: Can we be bought, with a higher salary, to compromise the Sabbath? The decision is of course personal and should be reached only with the Lord's help.

When my dad's parents were much younger, they used to own a hobby shop in Las Vegas that we kids loved to play in every time we visited them. It was only recently that I learned the extent of the financial risk they assumed near the beginning of their ownership because they determined to keep the Sabbath day holy.

My grandparents had known that this hobby shop was practically bankrupt before they looked it over as a possible purchase, but my grandpa had reviewed the books and found that the business was in trouble simply because no one had really minded the store. They mortgaged their home and bought the shop.

One of their first customers informed them that they would never make it if they didn't keep their store open on Sunday. He told them that Sunday is the best day for flying kites, model planes, etc., and that hobby enthusiasts needed the shop open in order to get parts. Grandpa told the man they wouldn't be open but that he should come in on Saturday and stock up. The customer replied, "You won't last very long."

Another customer, a man whose hobby was model trains, told them the same thing, received the same response, and as a result announced that he would start his own hobby business and keep it open seven days a week. His parting words were, "I will run you out of business."

That man did open shop, and for a while, my grandparents did miss many customers. They wondered how long they could continue. But then the customers started trickling back, and out of curiosity one day, Grandpa drove past the other store. It was closed—out of business! They don't know why, but perhaps it was simply from the owner's neglect. In any case, Grandpa's store, the Hobby Shop, open six days a week, remained in business until they retired thirty years later.

Most of my work with ESPN has been accomplished Monday through Saturday, due to a verbal agreement with my boss that if at all possible, I am not to be assigned to events on Sunday. Consequently, I have covered a lot of high school and college athletes, but rarely the pros. Two or three times a year I've had to fulfill my commitment by agreeing to work on Sunday. For instance, when I covered the French Open tennis championship in Paris, there was no way I could convince the Grand Slam officials to close down the courts on Sunday. I continued on with my reports.

But in 1989 I had to make a major decision. Strangely enough, it wasn't a hard decision to make at all. I was offered the opportunity of a lifetime—the kind of offer that anyone in my line of work strives for as the pinnacle of a career.

I had been assigned to interview Roberto Duran, the champion boxer from Panama, and then to cover his third fight against Sugar Ray Leonard in Las Vegas, the fight that was dubbed "Uno Más" by the press. I had never been to a fight before, much less reported on one, but I did my best.

The fight was lopsided, Sugar Ray winning rather easily. Following the bout, I had the assignment to interview Duran in his trailer. With about thirty people crammed into this small space, I was the first reporter to interview Roberto after the fight, and I began asking him questions, first in English (for our viewers) and then in Spanish (for Roberto). The interview went well, and in five minutes I was through with my assignment in Las Vegas.

The next morning I got a telephone call from the secretary for the president of NBC Sports, who wanted to know if I'd be willing to meet with him. *Would I be willing?* That was like asking me if I'd care for chocolate chip cookies fresh from the oven!

"Yes, of course," I said. "But what for, may I ask?"

"He would like to know if you're interested in a job," she replied coolly.

Somehow I managed to quell my excitement enough to suggest she give my agent a call, and I tried to sound professional as I said he handled all such requests. Outwardly, I may have sounded pretty cool, but inside I was almost giddy. *Wow! A job with a network, one of the Big Three!* I thought. I couldn't believe that I had actually been noticed by the upper echelons of the television industry.

I immediately called my agent, Michael Goldberg, in New York City, and asked him what I should make of it. He told me he wasn't sure, but that he would give them a call that minute.

After twiddling my thumbs in my hotel room for thirty minutes, I got a call back.

"Can you be in New York next week?" Michael asked.

"Are you kidding? What did they say?" was my attempt at a calm response.

Michael told me that NBC was interested in hiring me as a reporter to work weekends, sending live reports from around the country to Bob Costas in the studio. It sounded very high-profile and financially rewarding.

This opportunity came at an interesting time in my life. My husband, Bob, and I were living in Massachusetts but were planning to move back to Utah. We had been married two years and were anxious to start a family, and Bob was planning to open a physical therapy clinic. I was no longer interested in full-time employment, and I had found ESPN willing to accommodate my plans and schedule. I didn't think NBC would be quite so flexible. Honored as I was by the job offer, I reminded Michael of my priorities and told him I thought we should turn it down and not waste NBC's time with a meeting.

The next day, Michael called me again. He said NBC understood my criteria and had assured him that it wouldn't be a waste of time for me to come in and meet with Terry O'Neil, president of NBC Sports. With everything on the table and them fully aware of my priorities, I agreed to a meeting. I felt that even with so many limitations, there might somehow be a way to make it to the top of my profession.

The NBC Building in New York City is very daunting. I felt small and out of place going in there. But at the same time, a lot of good things had happened to me, and I had experienced some success. So though I was a little nervous, I felt confident.

Michael and I were ushered into Mr. O'Neil's office, where we waited for a few minutes. I was expecting to meet a commanding, high-powered, executive type, but instead I met a kind, charismatic individual who immediately put me at ease. After some small talk, Terry asked me what my professional goals were, which ordinarily wouldn't be a difficult question to answer. The logical response might be to "become the best" at sportscasting or "make it to the top!" But after getting married, I had changed my focus a great deal, and career goals didn't matter so much to me. I'm afraid my answer wasn't terribly sophisticated or impressive: "I enjoy working in a variety of sporting environments—I'm not necessarily partial only to the three main professional sports of basketball, football, and baseball—and I just want to have fun at whatever I do," I explained.

He seemed amused by my answer. Maybe he expected me to say I aspired to be the anchor of this hot show or the announcer for that spectacular event. He said that he understood that I didn't want to live in New York City (I nodded) and that I wanted to work part-time, so I could start a family (I nodded again). He told me that was no problem, because what they had in mind would only require me to work two days a week. I immediately perked up—just two days? I would fly to a variety of locations and feed live reports back to Bob Costas in the studio. Naturally, I smiled at the prospect—this *was* a "high-profile" job he was talking about. But there was a problem. The show was aired on weekends—Saturday and Sunday.

I told Terry I was flattered even to be considered but asked him just how many Sundays would be involved? He said virtually every Sunday of the year. Well, the decision was easy from there. I explained that I couldn't take a job that required me to work *every* Sunday. To my surprise, Terry smiled and said he knew exactly what I meant and that he was able to appreciate my position. My agent still wasn't sure if he had heard me right.

The meeting ended well, and I felt great, I suppose partly because I was so honored to have been given consideration for that kind of job, but more so because I hadn't compromised the things I had always believed in. I knew the job wasn't necessary as a means of feeding and clothing my family or providing security for them, and that meant there was only one appropriate answer for me to give—"No."

The question of what is or what is not appropriate to do on Sunday is a personal one. President James E. Faust of the First Presidency writes:

> Where is the line as to what is acceptable and unacceptable on the Sabbath? Within the guidelines, each of us must answer this question for ourselves. While these guidelines are contained in the scriptures and in the words of the modern prophets, they must also be written in our hearts and governed by our consciences. Brigham Young said of the faithful that "the spirit of their religion leaks out of their hearts" [in *Journal of Discourses,* 26 vols. [London: Latter-day Saints' Book Depot, 1854–86], 15:83]. It is quite unlikely that there will be any serious violation of Sabbath worship if we come humbly before the Lord and offer him all our heart, our soul, and our mind (see Matthew 22:37).
>
> On the Sabbath day we should do what we have to do and what we ought to do in an attitude of worshipfulness and then limit our other activities. *(Finding Light in a Dark World* [Salt Lake City: Deseret Book Company, 1995], pp. 115–16)

Earlier in the same chapter, President Faust reminds us that the Lord told Moses and the children of Israel, "Verily my sabbaths ye shall keep: for it is a sign between me and you throughout your generations . . . for a perpetual covenant. It is a sign between me and the children of Israel for ever" (Exodus 31:13, 16–17).

If we are going to be a beacon light to anyone, we must be consistent. Living the gospel six days out of seven is not enough, especially if the seventh is the Lord's day.

CHAPTER 7

OBJECTIONABLE SITUATIONS

I once gave a lesson to a Sunday School class of sixteen- and seventeen-year-olds on the topic of personal integrity, in which I asked this question: "What do you think the Lord would say if he were to make a short statement about you?" I passed around paper and pencils and asked the class members to write down an honest, soul-searching answer. They didn't have to sign their statements, and I hoped they would feel free to respond candidly. I should have known that when teenagers are given an opportunity to write whatever they want, and do so anonymously, well, it's as though they've just discovered "free speech."

The first response simply read, "Awesome." I have a feeling that person was unaware of the scripture that reads, "Be clothed with humility: for God resisteth the proud, and giveth grace to the humble. Humble yourselves therefore under the mighty hand of God, that he may exalt you in due time" (1 Peter 5:5–6).

The same scripture might well have been read by another student, who had written: "One of his most favorite kids . . . a real good guy with a small ego." Oh, well, given most teenagers' anxiety about their self-worth, I suppose humility is not a characteristic they are trying very hard to cultivate.

Most of the others wrote down the adjectives that

described their strengths instead of their weaknesses. They said the Lord would find them kind, loving, honest, true, patient, loyal, thoughtful of others' feelings, courageous, cheerful, sensitive, witty, smart, outgoing, resourceful, spiritual, optimistic, and respectful. Wow! I hadn't realized that I had the privilege of instructing a group that was so close to being translated!

When it comes right down to it, though, I guess we all desperately hope that the Lord will somehow overlook our weaknesses in favor of our strengths, and perhaps we feel it best not to remind him of our shortcomings. I suppose that's why I most admired the answers that indicated a willingness on the part of the writer to recognize his or her weaknesses.

"Struggling to define her beliefs and values, but walking in the right direction," one student wrote.

"Putting forth an effort—striving to become as He is," was another thoughtful response.

"Trying to do what's right," said another.

And my personal favorite: "He is a little confused, but he will straighten out."

I wouldn't be surprised if that last statement is, in fact, what the Lord would say about most of us, at least at some point in our lives. And, sometimes, that is what the battle is all about—just plugging away, relying on faith and a sense of right, even if you're not sure why, or how long it will take to get there.

After reading a few of the statements to the class, I turned to the scriptures for some examples of how the Lord has actually evaluated some of his servants:

"Blessed is my servant Hyrum Smith; for I, the Lord, love

him because of the integrity of his heart, and because he loveth that which is right before me, saith the Lord" (D&C 124:15).

"My servant George Miller is without guile; he may be trusted because of the integrity of his heart; and for the love which he has to my testimony I, the Lord, love him" (D&C 124:20).

It is impressive that one of the main reasons these two servants were loved and trusted was because of the integrity of their hearts.

Elder Bruce R. McConkie wrote, "The highest manifestation of integrity is exhibited by those who conform their conduct to the terms of those gospel covenants and promises which they have made" (*Mormon Doctrine,* 2d ed. [Salt Lake City: Bookcraft, 1966], p. 385). In other words (not that I could ever improve on Elder McConkie's words!), everything we say and do, *including* the environment we allow ourselves to be in, should be in complete harmony with those "covenants and promises" we have made. Our word *has* to be as good as gold, or else we have no integrity. And if we have no integrity, what then are we worth?

We can't always control the environment in which we find ourselves. For instance, it is difficult to do anything about a woman who swears at her child in the grocery store or to avoid seeing the many suggestive billboards, posters, and magazine covers that are displayed in public places. I may feel bothered or offended by such things, but I don't have to become "involved." I can simply ignore them and go on about my business.

But what happens when you can't simply ignore an unpleasant situation? What if you have a colleague who persists in swearing and telling off-color stories in your presence? What can you do if your boss directs you to do something unethical? What if your friends suggest going to a movie that is offensive or disgusting? In such cases, you can't just ignore what is happening. By not saying or doing anything, or by just going along with the crowd, you may give the impression that you approve and are willing to compromise your standards. It isn't only words that communicate. We shouldn't underestimate how easily our peers pick up on our nonverbal reactions and interpret from them what we really believe and value. Sometimes our silence, our body language, says as much about us as our words.

When I was barely twenty years old, I was suddenly faced with bookings for what seemed like an endless number of photo shoots. Most often they were on behalf of corporate sponsors of the Miss America pageant—for companies such as Gillette, Pillsbury, and so on. But there were quite a few for the media as well. Sometimes a wardrobe was provided for the shoot, and in those cases I would go through the available outfits and choose something to wear that was modest and conservative. I wasn't completely wise to the world yet, but I did know that the clothing I wore in those photos would speak volumes about me. What hadn't occurred to me was what my *pose* in the photo might suggest.

I recall one particular photo session in New York City. After several rolls of film had been taken, the photographer moved a couch onto the set and asked me to lie down on it for the photo. He and his crew had been pleasant to work with, and I felt I could trust him, so I listened as he described the shot he wanted. It seemed innocent enough. My dress was modest, and I was almost ready to comply when I was suddenly stopped by an image that flashed into my mind. I didn't like what I saw. It was a picture of someone trying to sell herself, of someone hoping to be liked and approved of by trying to appear seductive. In that split second, I knew I did not want to project any such image, and I told the photographer I would prefer to not lie down. I suggested I sit on the couch instead. He gave me a quizzical look but then shrugged his shoulders and said, "Okay."

Rather than make any attempt to look sexy in the pictures, I kept a friendly smile on my face. I decided that "come hither" poses simply weren't me. I would have looked unnatural and uncomfortable in such a photo, and it would not have conveyed what I preferred to have said about me.

That photo session was no big deal, and no fuss was made over my choice to sit rather than recline. But I did leave with a better sense of *my* ability and responsibility to control the image that I project. That and other experiences have helped me understand that if I want to stay clear of objectionable situations and avoid any misunderstanding about my level of commitment, I simply cannot afford to compromise—by my words, my actions, or my body language. There are times when the ability to compromise is an admirable trait—but compromising one's integrity is not one of them. Where integrity is involved, there can be no compromise.

Having said that, I'd like to make it clear that just because someone cherishes their integrity, that doesn't mean he or she has to be an overbearing, self-righteous, humorless person. No one likes or appreciates being around someone who is continually underlining or broadcasting their own virtue. A superior attitude is really unbecoming and can be irritating. Take a stand, but take an unpretentious, unassuming stand that will inspire those around you with a desire to be better. With that in mind, consider the following kinds of situations where we need to take a stand.

FOUL LANGUAGE. In the elementary, junior high, and high schools I attended, vulgarity and profanity were commonly heard. Sometimes foul language was used to insult others, sometimes just for shock value. It seemed to me the boys and young men who used that kind of language were trying to impress somebody, though I have no idea who—certainly not the girls, who were generally repulsed by that kind of speech. (Way back then, I rarely heard girls use obscene language.) I had no desire to be around people whose mouths seemed to emit a never-ending stream of filth, and I can still remember the names of the worst offenders.

After we had all grown up, one of those boys I had often heard swear asked me out on a date. Even though he might have discovered a dictionary by then and replaced his vulgar speech with something less offensive, I had no desire to go out with him. It had nothing to do with forgiveness, it was just a matter of personal preference. My childhood opinion of him had sort of stuck with me. His language had given me no reason to like or admire him.

Of course, obscene speech is not just a childhood phenomenon. It occurs in all age groups and at all socioeconomic levels. In fact, in many settings in the world it is almost impossible to avoid hearing vulgar or obscene speech, and unless a person is determined, it's difficult to refrain from mimicking it. Maybe it's a little bit like the "valley girl" dialect, which is characterized by distinctive voice inflections and the use of repetitive expressions such as "like, you know," "for sure," and "totally." I've heard that many people (teenagers in particular) who move into an area where "valley girl" is spoken soon adopt that pattern of speech. Likewise, vulgar and obscene speech patterns almost seem to be infectious. The best way to deal with foul language is to avoid it.

But what do you do when you can't avoid it? For instance, consider the workplace. In an effort to underscore their authority or command the attention of their employees, some bosses use offensive language. And subordinates frequently use the same kind of language to express frustration or give the illusion of their own importance. We aren't always able to avoid hearing vulgar or obscene words. How should we respond?

I have often been in these kinds of situations, but one in particular was when I was given my first assignment with ESPN as a sideline reporter at the 1987 Holiday Bowl, as I mentioned earlier. My boss was a young but highly respected producer who was gaining a reputation for being innovative, aggressive, and extremely competent. I was glad to hear all that, since I didn't feel particularly competent in this, my first time in front of a national television audience as a reporter. I needed all the help I could get.

In preparation for the broadcast, I met with the producer and the play-by-play and color commentary announcers a couple of times for several hours to go over our television game plan. I began to feel comfortable with my new colleagues, and they put me at ease by telling me they had confidence in my abilities. Finally, it was game time, and I headed for the sidelines, a bit scared but feeling fairly confident.

The first half went relatively well, but in the second half I made a rookie mistake that made us all look bad. I was interviewing a former NFL star who was an alumnus of one of the college teams on the field, when suddenly the crowd erupted. Standing with my back to the field, I didn't know what was happening. I was intent on completing my interview. I should have said, "We'll come back to you in a minute—right now let's go to Jim for the action." But knowing exactly what to do when you're caught off guard is a skill that comes with experience, and I was relatively new on the job.

So, instead, I continued to talk to this ex-player, oblivious to the breakaway, sixty-yard touchdown run that had just turned the stadium inside out. Of course, the producer made sure that our viewers at home were watching the play, not me, but instead of a description of the action on the field, they heard me and the former NFL star talking about his good ol' days in college. I was made aware of my goof when the producer yelled into my headset during a break. But he didn't have time to elaborate, so I knew I would hear about it after the game. Naturally, I was embarrassed, and I tried hard to make sure my performance during the rest of the game was flawless.

Following the game, I went back to the truck where the producer sits to direct the telecast. As soon as he was free, I began my apology but was immediately cut short. He lit into me with a barrage of unmentionable words that at first stunned me because of how angry he was, but which very quickly began to offend me. I didn't deserve to be treated that way, no matter how badly I had performed.

When he paused to catch his breath, I said to him, "You don't have to speak to me that way. If that's your way of trying to get me to perform better, you need to learn something about human relations—I don't respond well when you address me that way; in fact, I don't respond at all. I know I made a mistake, but your rudeness doesn't change anything—it just makes me angry." I left before he could respond with any of the words he might have left out of his first tirade. He later apologized and blamed his behavior on the heat of the moment.

Working as a sports telecaster can be hectic. The language used by the broadcast crew is often coarse, especially when the pressure mounts, as in the example of my first producer. Still, FCC regulations require a certain on-air decorum, so most of the colorful language gets used during commercial breaks and when the announcers get a chance to air their grievances to the producer, the director, the technicians, or to whomever might have fouled up. Generally, that isn't a problem, *unless* someone forgets to turn off a microphone. Then the viewers (especially viewers of satellite transmissions) get an unexpected earful. That possibility makes TV executives nervous. They don't like having to worry about someone they've hired saying something vulgar or offensive that might go out over the airwaves. I get a chuckle out of the irony of this standard: profanity or vulgarity is tolerated, even accepted, everywhere but on the air.

I recall one of those instances. I was standing on the sideline listening in my headset to everyone going berserk because some foul language had indeed escaped the confines of the announcers' booth. I was standing next to the field producer, who leaned over and said to me, "Well, they sure won't ever have to worry about bleeping anything that comes out of your mouth—unless, of course, 'Oh, my goodness,' and 'heck' make it onto the dirty laundry list." It was a good-natured teasing that I didn't mind at all.

I have often been kidded by my colleagues about my "alternative" choice of words, but at least I won't lose a job because I can't control the expletives that come out of my mouth. In a world that scarcely recognizes there even *is* such a thing as profanity, I realize that using my "alternative" words to express surprise or exasperation exposes me to the risk of sounding a little silly, but I'm willing to take that risk. And when I run across someone else who refuses to use profanity, it's refreshing and brightens my day.

I'm pleasantly amazed that network TV still bothers to bleep out offensive language. Given the rest of the trash they are willing to broadcast, it's especially surprising. I guess there is still a standard of decency, which gives me hope.

In our everyday encounters with foul language, it is usually best to simply walk away from it. People will get the idea that you are offended by vulgarity and obscenity. If you intend to rebuke everyone who uses offensive language, you'd better find a comfortable soapbox, since you'll be standing on it several hours a day. But if the language is particularly offensive—such as that used by the producer who offended me—then it should be addressed, especially if the language is unusually profane and sacrilegious.

The use of profanity is without question a problem both within and outside Church membership. One way that "good" members of the Church often feel justified in swearing is when quoting someone or simply trying to emphasize a point. It *should* go without saying that swearing is never justified.

Sometimes, there are those who—for reasons only they

know—become so accustomed to using expletives that they may not realize how their actions are affecting those around them. It takes courage to let them know, and while many of us might strike out as we take a swing, every now and then we'll make a hit. A few years ago I heard Dale Murphy give a fireside at Brigham Young University in which he said something that would apply here: "When I'm in a slump, I just keep swinging hard . . . in case I hit something!"

When my husband was a senior in high school, one of the school's most popular leaders was known to occasionally use profanity and participate in "locker room talk." As a member of the Church in this predominantly LDS student body, this young man was in a position to influence a lot of kids with his poor example. The LDS seminary council became concerned, since his actions had the potential to affect a great number of students. They decided to simply approach the young man and ask him to change his behavior.

Because my husband has always been known for being completely honest and direct with people, he was given the assignment to talk to his classmate about being a better example. A little nervous, Bob approached the student leader in the locker room after physical education class. Nearly everyone had cleared out, and the two were able to talk quietly. Later, I read in Bob's yearbook about the effect of that conversation (which I include despite Bob's modest reluctance!):

"Bob, it seems like just yesterday that you and I were sitting in the locker room talking. I hope that I made some change in the right direction of improvement. I guess you will be the most respected guy in the whole school because you have done nothing to disgrace your name or your priesthood. Bob, you are a special person and I know that you will always have a successful life because of your faithfulness to our Heavenly Father. I'm going to miss watching your face in the locker room after somebody swore or told a dirty joke. Well, I don't know if I will ever gain the respect from the rest of the people as much as you have, but it will always give me a goal to strive for." It was signed, "Your friend forever."

That note said as much about the writer as it did in its praise of Bob. Instead of becoming defensive, this young man took a closer look at his actions and how they might be affecting others. Consequently, he decided to make a change. Today, as the bishop of his ward, he is the positive role model he was meant to be. I have no doubt the locker-room chat with Bob was inspired.

Joseph Smith provided us a powerful example of confronting those who offend. While he was being unjustly held in prison in Richmond, Missouri, the guards tormented their Mormon prisoners for hours with their foul-mouthed, vulgar boasts of how they had abused the Mormon people they had been persecuting. The Prophet Joseph had finally had all he could stand. Parley P. Pratt, who had been lying next to Joseph on the floor, recalled, "On a sudden he arose to his feet, and spoke in a voice of thunder, or as the roaring lion, uttering, as near as I can recollect, the following words:

"'*SILENCE, ye fiends of the infernal pit. In the name of Jesus Christ I rebuke you, and command you to be still; I will not live another minute and hear such language. Cease such talk, or you or I die THIS INSTANT!*'" (*Autobiography of Parley P. Pratt* [Salt Lake City: Deseret Book Company, 1985], pp. 179–80).

Of course, we probably aren't going to respond quite that

forcefully, but there may be times when we will need to say something rather than continue to listen to language that offends us. Usually, people who use gross language halfway suspect they are out of line. They may be embarrassed to be confronted, but there isn't any way they can justify themselves for speaking like that, and you don't have to be afraid to say something that will remind them to behave more courteously. Remembering Joseph Smith's bold example may give you the courage to speak up when it becomes necessary.

Another example of one who never backs down (whether on or off the field!) is Jason Buck, the 1987 Outland Trophy winner from BYU. After college, Jason went on to play professional football. He happens to be from my husband's hometown of St. Anthony, Idaho, so we have known Jason and his wife, Roxi, for years, and we've always admired their consistent dedication to gospel principles, no matter what the circumstance.

One day Jason and I were talking about the prevalence of foul language on and around the football field. We agreed that because it is so commonplace, we've had to pretty much learn to ignore it and just let our example speak for itself. But even though we were both involved with the game, Jason's situation was obviously quite different from my own. Most people don't expect a woman to let out a string of swear words, but football players are perceived differently. There is a tendency to link a foul mouth with hard-nosed, aggressive play.

When Jason played for the Cincinnati Bengals, some of the coaches and players alike actually questioned his commitment to the game, simply because he was a family man who took seriously his responsibility to be a role model. Because he didn't use four-letter words in his conversation, some wondered if he was aggressive or tough enough; it was impossible for them to understand there is absolutely no correlation between the two.

During a lull in a team meeting one day, one of the more vocal players was talking about his usual subjects that ranged from descriptions of his status as a ladies' man to his agnostic or atheistic points of view. He was being his typical, crude self, but this time he pushed it too far. He went beyond disgusting vulgarity and began using the Lord's name in vain in a particularly offensive way.

In the three years Jason had known the player, he had never heard him spout off *so* crudely. Having heard enough, Jason turned to him and said, "Don't you ever speak that way anywhere near me again. I believe in God the Eternal Father and his Son, Jesus Christ, and I won't tolerate that kind of speech coming out of you or anyone else. I've always respected your beliefs—now you respect mine."

The small room had suddenly turned quiet. The other player sat there with his mouth open, but this time, silent. He never said anything remotely vulgar or profane in front of Jason again, and neither did the other guys who had heard the rebuke. Whether they internalized the lesson or not, they came away with a better understanding that *meek* most certainly does not mean *weak*. In fact, if anything, you must be stronger than all the others in order to stand alone.

When Jason was traded to the Washington Redskins, he found himself in a more compatible environment. Many of his teammates there shared his Christian beliefs and lived a similar code of conduct. He was never teased about his standards, and no one ever called into question his aggressiveness. As a member of that team, Jason earned a Super Bowl ring, which more than proves there is no correlation between the use of foul language and the competitive fire it takes to become a champion.

DIRTY JOKES AND STORIES. One of the most uncomfortable social situations for me is created when a friend or a colleague begins to tell an off-color joke. What should I do? Should I laugh to be polite, or is it better to register my disapproval in some way?

I've found that it is best not to make a big deal of it. It's not necessary to laugh at something you don't find amusing. After all, that's a kind of hypocrisy itself. Sometimes it is best to just ignore it or find something better to do. Our friends are probably smart enough to catch on. No one enjoys trying to be a stand-up comedian to an audience that isn't responding, and when the joke teller discovers that a particular kind of story isn't funny to some people, it takes the fun out of telling it.

My husband, Bob, was on his high school's wrestling and football teams, and since he lived in a small town, these teams often had to travel long distances by bus to get to their matches and games. As on most team buses, the more experienced and popular players would gravitate to the back of the bus, and that is where most of the entertainment for the road trip could be found. Bob says he usually started out sitting in the back, until the recitation of dirty jokes began. At that point, he'd simply stand up and casually say to no one in particular, "Wow, my ears are too sensitive for that stuff," and then he'd move up the aisle out of earshot. Everyone would chuckle with him as they got the gentle but obvious hint.

He didn't pass judgment on anyone, nor did he take himself too seriously. In essence, he teased himself for being (in the eyes of his buddies) prudish. He never lost any friends even though he refused to listen. He was always "one of the guys," and he never gave the impression that he was too good for them. But he made it clear that he wouldn't compromise his views to be exactly like them—or to be liked by them.

My Uncle Kenneth is a retired commercial airline pilot who was an officer in the United States Air Force during both World War II and the Korean Conflict. During the war years, he grew used to hearing inappropriate language and the dirty jokes that were so much a part of that kind of life. Though he never used such language (and never condoned it), he reluctantly recognized that it was as much a part of military life as the dog tags he wore for identification.

But Uncle Kenneth was well known for having strong opinions. And he always said exactly what he thought, without concern for whether or not he was being "politically correct." As an officer, he found that the men quickly responded to his comments and tried to comply with his requests, at least while he was around.

One time, while the men in his squadron were all relaxing, the conversation turned to a common subject: the telling and retelling of their female conquests. Uncle Kenneth didn't waste any time interrupting them.

"Why is it that when women do what you say they do, you call them degrading names. But when *you* are involved with these women of questionable character, you brag about it?" he asked pointedly.

After that, Uncle Kenneth didn't hear any more tales of

conquest—the men simply didn't include him in their story-telling hour, an arrangement he found to his liking.

Following his years in the air force, Uncle Kenneth went to work as a pilot for a commercial airline. His routes took him on long flights to all parts of the world, and as Captain Kenneth Walser of a DC-8, his orders to the crew were respected and quickly obeyed, just as they had been when he was an officer in the military. He also discovered that civilian personnel are just as capable of telling off-color stories as servicemen are and that men aren't the only ones who have a dirty joke to tell.

On one of his flights, the senior flight attendant was a woman with whom Uncle Kenneth had not previously worked, although she had worked with some of the other members of his crew. She would occasionally visit the flight deck to keep the crew informed if something had to be taken care of in the cabin. But one time she paid a strictly social visit to the cockpit, and hoping to ingratiate herself with the flight crew, began telling what she thought was a funny story.

As soon as Uncle Kenneth caught the gist of the story, he interrupted her and rather curtly asked her if she didn't have something to do back in the cabin. She got the message and promptly left, leaving the rest of the story untold. Captain Walser then told the flight engineer that the woman was not to be allowed on deck again. If she had something to report, he was to take the message and then she was to immediately return to the cabin.

The flight engineer probably told the flight attendant why she had been banned from the cockpit, because after the flight, she approached Uncle Kenneth and apologized. After that incident, she was assigned to his crew on a number of occasions and was always perfectly respectful; her comments were always appropriate whenever she was in his presence. Word quickly spread, and he had no problems with anyone else in that regard.

For many of us, it would be difficult to take such a strong stand for the reason that it would immediately set us apart, even alienate us from our peer group. There's no question that the dirty jokes would continue to be told, just not in our presence, and we might fear becoming self-made "loners" because of our intolerance. I remember one of my sisters making a nonsensical statement to our mother one time when Mom questioned her choice of outrageous school clothing. In frustration, my sister said, "I want to be an individual, just like everybody else!" We all got a chuckle out of it because the paradox was so obvious. So which is it? Do we prefer being an individual or do we want to be just like everyone else? We can't have it both ways. People who ultimately earn their peers' respect are those who take an unwavering stand for right.

The summer my mother graduated from Brigham Young University, she and a girlfriend went to Alaska for an adventurous three months to work at a resort hotel—Mount McKinley Park Hotel—located in the Denali Park at the base of Mount McKinley.

They were housed in a dormitory with other college-age young women. Sometimes, after work, the young men who were working there would join the girls in the dorm's recreation room, and they enjoyed sharing with each other funny stories, jokes, their experiences with the tourists, and so on. Some of the jokes, though, were a little off-color, and the language, at times, was not very appropriate.

These two LDS girls would quietly excuse themselves and leave the group. One day, one of the other members of the group asked my mother why she and her friend didn't stay longer sometimes, and my mom told her that the stories and the language were offensive to them and they just preferred to not listen.

This person, along with another girl and her fiancé (who was also working at the hotel), were so impressed with the values of these two LDS women that they wanted to know more about what they believed. My mom and her friend taught the gospel to their three new friends after work each night, and at the end of the summer all three were baptized when they returned to their homes. Three lives changed because of the example of two young women who realized the importance of living the Lord's standards, no matter how far away from home they were or with whom they associated.

On occasion, the conversations we find ourselves swept into might not be considered "dirty," but they present still other problems. People, whether members of the Church or not, have a tendency to want to share stories of personal encounters with evil influences—perhaps as a way of entertainment around a campfire or at a slumber party. They share them for a variety of reasons. But such stories just provide another opportunity to reinvite the evil influence back into the lives of the storyteller and those listening. We must keep our conversations and thoughts uplifting at all times if we are to be led by the Spirit.

QUESTIONABLE ENTERTAINMENT. Here's a situation that has become even trickier for me to handle in recent years, partly because I know so many people (both nonmembers and Latter-day Saints) who are willing to compromise on the issue of entertainment. More and more people accept whatever the entertainment industry creates, even if the material is graphically obscene. Though our Church leaders have repeatedly admonished us to stay away from R-rated movies, many Latter-day Saints choose to ignore the counsel, and they make some compelling (and often impassioned) arguments in favor of some of these films. In an attempt to rationalize their attendance, these people point out that a particular movie won a major award or that there is only a brief suggestive scene or that there is just a small amount of violence or offensive language in it. Some defend movies that are rated R "just for violence," implying that although it's unacceptable to view sexual scenes, it's all right to watch scenes of torture, bloodshed, warfare, and murder. Such arguments are particularly difficult to resist when the subject matter is otherwise uplifting or inspiring. (Something else I find equally intriguing is the number of Church members who don't go to R-rated movies in the theater and yet somehow feel justified renting them in video stores to view in the privacy of their own homes. It's as if R-rated *videos* are somehow less offensive than R-rated *movies.* Is it just me, or is personal integrity at issue here?)

My husband and I have found a way to deal with this issue, and it is very simple. Rather than debate the merits of one film or another, we have chosen to avoid viewing *anything* that is R-rated. For us, it has become simply a matter of principle rather than a topic to be discussed. We have found it is a whole lot easier to distinguish between black and white than it is some shades of gray.

But our having drawn a line doesn't make it any less

awkward when we want to go see a movie with friends. More often than not, the most talked-about, most thrilling film being shown is R-rated. So, to avoid all that, we make plans to see a movie with friends only when we can choose a G- or PG-rated film that has received great reviews and seems to be popular at the box office.

It ought to be enough that our leaders have warned us against viewing R-rated films. But there is something else to be considered. Viewing such movies and sitting through multiple depictions of sex or violence eventually dulls our sensitivity to such things and fills our minds with images that are all too easy to recall. A study was released and reported on the nightly news (KSL-TV [NBC], 5 February 1996) that stated that 73 percent of the sex or violence depicted on TV resulted in *no* consequences in the story line. In other words, no matter how "realistic" the scenes may be made to appear, no consequences of these scenes are shown. Most of us have already noticed that: for example, a "good" main character kills someone, but the TV program doesn't go on to show the tragic consequences to the victim's family, etc. In fact, after sitting for a couple of hours watching close-ups of beautiful, charismatic characters, we find it difficult to feel hostile toward them or to condemn their behavior—no matter how bizarre or immoral it may be. Hollywood is very skillful at making evil to appear good. Just remember, though, *it's their job to convince you.* After all . . . *they're actors!*

I'm not in Las Vegas very often, but since my dad is originally from that area and many of his relatives still live there, I am quite familiar with both the positives and negatives of that brightly lit city. And because Dad has such fond memories of

his childhood there, most of what I have heard has been positive. Only occasionally have I been reminded that there is a
darker side to the city. It seems almost symbolic to me that the
Las Vegas Temple is located next to the mountains and as far
away from the "Strip" as it could be and still be in the city.

In December 1992, ESPN assigned me to work as the sideline reporter for the inaugural Las Vegas Bowl, featuring two
of the top Division II college football teams. I was there for
three days, and at the end of a very long first day during which
I had interviewed a number of players, one of the bowl officials
asked me and the others on the production team if we would
be interested in seeing a show that night. He said he could get
us complimentary tickets to anything that hadn't already been
sold out. Well, with such short notice, there was hardly anything to choose from, but he did get back to us with one rec-
ommendation for that evening. Since I was familiar enough
with "Las Vegas" type shows, I asked him specifically if there
was any nudity of any kind in this show. He assured me it was a
variety show that catered to families—that there was absolutely
no nudity in the production—and besides (he added with the
confidence of a true Las Vegas native), those kinds of shows
were found more often *off* the Strip these days. According to
him, the really popular entertainments were quite clean. Even
after all that, I again asked him if he was 100 percent positive,
because I had absolutely no desire to attend a show in which
the costumes played second fiddle. He said he was positive. I
should have known better.

As it turned out, my producer and I were the only ones in
our crew who finished up in time to make it to the 7:00 show.
We rushed in and sat down just as the lights in the room were

dimming. I was tired, so I was looking forward to sitting back and being entertained.

The orchestra began and the stage lights came up. The featured performer, a male singer, descended from the risers on stage. His rhinestone-studded jacket caught every beam of light and it sparkled as he sang. He worked his way through a standard repertoire of "Feelings" and "You Are the Sunshine of My Life," in a style that reminded me of performers I had seen on *The Love Boat* on TV—competent but bland. Surrounding him onstage was an ensemble of dancers dressed in feathers, beads, and sequins.

The show was proving to be just standard. The singers weren't exceptional, and the dancers functioned as not much more than clothes hangers for their elaborate costumes. The mediocrity of the whole thing was disguised behind typical Las Vegas glitz—extravagant lighting and loud music.

After sitting through five minutes of this, I had resigned myself to giving up and just enduring the production. My producer was from the East and had never seen a Las Vegas show before, and I guessed he might find it interesting. But since the show featured such lackluster performers and average dancers, it wasn't likely to be very entertaining.

Then, suddenly, out of nowhere and for no apparent reason, a line of about eight women paraded onstage, wearing yards and yards of decorations on their heads but precious little else to cover the rest of their bodies. After having received repeated assurances from the bowl official that the show included no such thing, I was shocked. But, as I said before, I should have known better.

The nearly nude performers left the stage almost as quickly

as they had arrived, and I breathed a sigh of relief. *Maybe that was just a token appearance and that's all there'll be,* I thought to myself. Our seats were right down in front, in the center of the theater, and I really didn't want to make a spectacle of myself by leaving. But, sure enough, the same ladies soon strolled back onto the stage, without contributing anything to the production whatsoever.

I was decidedly uncomfortable, so I leaned over to my producer and told him that I hoped he wouldn't mind but that I was leaving. To my surprise, he nodded his head, agreeing with me, and said he would leave with me! We worked our way over to the wall, but it was dark and we couldn't find an exit. We chose a door and soon found ourselves, not in the hotel lobby, but in a service hallway that led to the kitchen! After meandering through a maze of hallways, we finally walked through a door into the parking lot.

I was surprised that my producer hadn't been eager to stay. I thought for sure he would have found such entertainment . . . well, entertaining. But as we discussed the show, he said he had been offended by the pointless display of near-nudity and he hadn't felt the show was worth watching. I agreed with him but felt even more strongly than he did. I thought it was garbage. In any case, it was gratifying to have my producer's support.

I hadn't had it in mind to chide the bowl official for recommending the show. I didn't want to embarrass him, and he had worked hard to make sure we enjoyed our stay in Las Vegas. But he somehow found out about my shocked reaction to the show (my producer must have said something). He apologized profusely for misleading me and said he would never let it happen again.

In this, the "information age," computers have even entered the stage as a form of entertainment. In fact, since anyone with a computer that is hooked up to the Internet has easy access to information on literally any subject, our society is currently debating whether or not there should be some measure of control over the amount and degree of information the general public (and that includes kids) may request. As with TV and the movies, "the Net" now includes offensive material of all kinds. A good friend of mine shared this valuable lesson he learned when fooling around with the computer gimmicks he had access to.

My friend, who we'll call Jim, worked in a profitable business with a few other men who shared his moral standards. One time, as he was trying to get some information off the computer, he inadvertently pulled up a photo of a beautiful girl wearing a skimpy swimsuit. Well, thinking he would get a chuckle out of his partners, who were every bit as "straight-laced" as he, Jim put the photo onto a screensaver so when his colleagues turned on their computers, they would see the photo and all would have a good laugh. He entered it, left the office, and forgot all about it—until the next day when he had a very important client in his office.

Jim had to show his client some documents on the computer, and as soon as he hit the key, the screensaver photo popped up on the screen. The client, who had known Jim for some time, did not hide his astonishment.

"I guess I'm a little surprised, Jim. I've always held you up as my role model of high moral standards," he said.

Jim told me, "It was like a swift kick in the head. I was embarrassed beyond belief."

He later told his colleagues what had happened, using that experience as an opportunity to remind all three how important actions are. "When we proclaim who we are, we have a responsibility to act accordingly. I didn't realize that my client had such a high opinion of me," Jim said. As he related this story to me, I immediately thought of something Elder Neal A. Maxwell once said: "Let us . . . not write checks with our tongues which our conduct cannot cash" ("A More Determined Discipleship," *Ensign,* February 1979, p. 70).

A couple of weeks later, Jim gathered up his courage and in humility called on the client he had so disillusioned. Jim thanked him for his friendship and honesty, admitted that the incident had had an impact on him, and expressed a renewed commitment to live even better.

As Latter-day Saints, we should have a pretty good idea of what is offensive or inappropriate entertainment. The question is, Have we *decided* what to do about it when we are confronted with it? To listen to or sit through something is the same as condoning it, and the more we are exposed to such things, the more accepting we become. It is possible to reach a point where we can no longer see the harm in offensive materials. Alexander Pope described it this way:

> Vice is a monster of so frightful mien,
> As to be hated needs but to be seen;
> Yet seen too oft, familiar with her face,
> We first endure, then pity, then embrace.
> (*An Essay on Man,* epistle 2, lines 217–20)

GAMBLING. Speaking of Las Vegas and questionable entertainment, surprisingly enough, gambling is a big problem for some Church members who think nothing of throwing away fifteen or twenty dollars and chalking it up to entertainment. Is playing the lottery or even playing bingo harmful? Before I quote the leaders of the Church on this topic, I must share my experience with the gambling industry.

When I traveled back to Atlantic City (the "Las Vegas" of the East Coast) for the Miss America pageant, we were given a set of rules for the week. Near the top was the rule that no contestant was to be found anywhere near the casinos—no cards, no tables, no machines. Why? We were told it would not reflect well on the pageant. Well, as members of the Church, shouldn't we be even more responsible towards that which we represent?

"No member of the Church of Jesus Christ of Latter-day Saints can afford to do himself the dishonor or to bring upon himself the disgrace, of crossing the threshold of a liquor saloon or a gambling [hall], or of any house of ill-fame of whatever name or nature it may be. No Latter-day Saint, no member of the Church can afford it, for it is humiliating to him, it is disgraceful in him to do it, and God will judge him according to his works" (Joseph F. Smith in Conference Report, October 1908, p. 7).

INAPPROPRIATE WORK ENVIRONMENTS. To a certain degree, we *can* control our environment, even our *working* environment. One of the more heated topics of debate in my workplace is the question of whether or not female reporters ought to be permitted access to men's locker rooms. My feeling is that women should not be in the men's locker room any more than men ought to be in women's changing areas. It's really that simple. In fact, I believe the locker room ought to be a private environment in which *no* reporters are admitted.

For me, this hasn't become a serious problem. My involvement has been mostly with high school and collegiate athletes or athletes of the highest caliber from sports that are less visible than football, baseball, and basketball. The athletes I have interviewed have usually been very accessible. In fact, I have often talked to them while they were in uniform.

However, about two years into my contract with ESPN, I was sent to shoot a feature on a couple of professional basketball players who were in the midst of the NBA play-offs. I needed to get the players' reactions immediately following the game, and that meant conducting a locker-room interview. Knowing that would be the case, I had told my producer well before the game that I would not be going into the locker room, and I gave him a list of questions I wanted him to ask the players. He said that would be fine. But I can see the dilemma faced by a female newspaper or magazine reporter who must meet a deadline, who doesn't have a producer nearby to help her out in that way. Still, change comes about when people demand a change and demand it long enough.

Individuals who work in worldly environments may sometimes get to the point where they are incapable of recognizing evil. I had a good friend who in school was generally thought of as a "goody-goody," even by LDS standards. I admired and respected her, not only for her remarkable talents but for the strength of her testimony. I knew that if anyone could be successful out in the "real world," yet remain faithful to all she believed, it would be her.

We didn't see each other for a number of years, but I was happy to watch her indeed become a big success in her chosen field. When we next saw each other we didn't have a chance to really talk much. As far as I knew, she was still active in the Church and had retained her original values, but as we visited I couldn't help noticing her immodest clothing and the comments she made about her new friends and the success she was enjoying. Her attitude made me wonder if she hadn't abandoned some of the things she had previously valued.

By the time we said good-bye, it almost felt as though she were dismissing me. I had the feeling that I had served as an unwelcome reminder of another time when her goals and purpose in life had been quite different.

I only mention the experience to point out that when we immerse ourselves in certain worldly environments, it is very difficult to avoid absorbing the things that surround us. Under those conditions, it is hard to stay focused on eternal values and goals. A testimony is a tender commodity, and no matter how strong it may be at a given point, it needs to be continually nurtured in an environment where the Spirit can influence us, or it may wither.

To balance the "real world" in which most of us spend much of our time, we can choose to frequently place ourselves in a sheltered environment where we can be nurtured by the Spirit. My parents helped our family find that balance throughout the many years when we were surrounded by those of other faiths, or of no faith at all. Many, many families do the same.

Keeping our spiritual balance is sometimes a matter of going out of our way to seek a spiritually nurturing environment, as my younger sister Elayne once learned. She once believed that to strengthen one's testimony, one must be in a challenging environment, surrounded by those with lower standards. That's how we had grown up, experiencing firsthand the growth of our testimonies as we constantly defended them. When Elayne was a student at Stanford University, she told me that she reasoned it was too easy to become complacent when one was surrounded only by people who believed the same. If there are challenges, she pointed out, surely one can rise above them and thus become a stronger person. Certainly there is some truth in that. As members of the Church, we look on trials as our "tests of faith," to make us stronger and better.

But when Elayne took a break from her English studies at Stanford to spend six months in Israel with the BYU study-abroad program, she reconsidered her position of voluntarily placing herself in swampy wetlands instead of on higher, drier ground. With her permission, I'd like to include an excerpt from the article she wrote for the LDS newsletter at Stanford:

> Sitting here on the shores of the Sea of Galilee, having just spent two weeks studying only the Savior and His teachings, I reflect on how easy it is to live the gospel and remain spiritually in tune when one is surrounded by only good forces. For two weeks the only books I have read have been scriptures and commentaries by the apostles. I have listened to no rock music, watched no TV, and associated only with people who are trying equally as hard to pattern their lives after Christ.
>
> But lest this sound as though I am seeking kudos or pats on the back, I only relate this to illustrate how easy it's been for me, in these surroundings, to become completely dedicated to the gospel and to doing the Lord's will. But a nagging feeling in the back of my head makes me wonder, how good is this "easiness" for me? Will the goals I have set in such an atmosphere be as strongly etched in my heart when

I am no longer here? Will they stand up to the difficulties and pressures of the "real world," i.e., Stanford?

I once shunned easiness for precisely these reasons—I feared that a tendency to seek out only "uplifting" atmospheres was indicative of weakness, a lack of courage to face adversity and temptations. Thus, I actively sought challenges—people who believed and lived differently than I, situations in which I would be tempted—foolishly believing that such an environment would make me a stronger person. Eventually, my insistence on being surrounded by challenges greatly overshadowed my desire to be influenced by good forces, and the means by which I had planned to become a stronger person were self-defeating.

Since then, and particularly in these two weeks, I have come to the conclusion that there is nothing wrong with seeking out atmospheres which make it easier for us to live the gospel. I still believe that spiritual challenges are good for us, in certain doses, and that they should not be fled from, but I don't think they should be actively sought, either. They will no doubt present themselves to us of their own accord.

My Miss America year—my whole life, for that matter—has taught me that no matter where we live, there are good influences and bad influences—and we are always surrounded by both. I believe it's good to seek adventure, even "spiritual" adventure (as my dad calls it) out in the geographical areas where Latter-day Saints are the minority, not the majority. But it's quite another thing to seek out the evil influences in the very same area. Yes, overcoming challenges does make us stronger, but as Elayne wrote, choosing the wrong influences is certainly "self-defeating," and choosing wholesome, nurturing spiritual influences is vital to our testimonies. When we're out in the "real world"—the rough, challenging atmosphere where faithlessness is prevalent—we can keep our balance only by recharging our spiritual batteries frequently. Whether it's getting together with even a small group of faithful Latter-day Saint friends, attending all our Church meetings, going to the temple often, or spending six months in Israel walking where the Savior walked, we grow stronger when we actively seek the shelter of wholesome, godly environments.

Have you ever noticed how the older people get, the more they set their own agenda and do things the way they want and when they want? Especially *really* old folks? They feel they have reached a point in life when they deserve it—they have earned the right to do what they want with their lives. And they have! I suggest we incorporate just a little of that attitude, mix it with some humility and a spirit of cooperation, then set the standards for our living and working environments. Just as the citizens of this nation have finally convinced smokers to light up outside the workplace, we can invite other things that are offensive and degrading to likewise step outside.

CHAPTER 8

"HOW MANY MOTHERS
DO YOU HAVE?"

No matter where you live or travel, people are bound to be curious when they discover you are a Mormon, and many of them will ask questions. It is impossible to outguess any preconceived notions they might have, but the first clue that they are misinformed about the Church might be their first question, such as "How many mothers do you have?"

Have you ever been asked a question like that? I have. I'll be talking with some well-meaning but misinformed person, and when they discover I'm a Mormon, they'll ask an unusual question such as how many mothers I have. Usually, I laugh and say, "Oh, just the normal number. How many do *you* have?" As strange as it seems, that little exchange has sometimes led to a lengthier conversation about the Church and my beliefs.

My dear friend whom I mentioned earlier, Rebecca (Becki) Simpson, once worked at the Visitors and Convention Bureau in Salt Lake City. She told me that the question she was asked most often (and usually asked in hushed tones!) was an amusing one: "What does a Mormon *look* like?" Well, such a question was simply too tempting to pass up. Mimicking their hushed tones, Becki would tell them to watch out for the ones with horns, or the ladies in the long pioneer dresses. Then with a warm smile she would say, "Actually, you're looking at one!" Since Becki is a beautiful, sophisticated, and intelligent woman, they would first register surprise, then embarrassment at their ignorance.

It is crucial, when fielding a seemingly dumb question, to not take offense. I've found that by responding with a sense of humor and a friendly manner you can turn that kind of a situation into an opportunity to explain the Church and its doctrines.

In this and the following two chapters, I will take a look at many of the questions I have been asked over the years by journalists, acquaintances, and friends of other faiths. From my teenage years in Argentina to the Miss America year and subsequently the years with ESPN, I can't imagine anything I *haven't* been asked. And I am constantly working on better ways to listen carefully to the question and not be surprised or thrown off by it, so that I may respond clearly and confidently. Perhaps you have responded, or will have to respond, to similar questions. I sincerely hope these ideas will serve to strengthen your expertise in handling any question.

Sometimes the questions I have been asked about the Church insinuate criticism: "Isn't Mormonism a cult?" or "Why do you collect the names of dead people? That sounds sinister to me!" And then there are the inevitable questions about polygamy, African-Americans and their status in the Church, and the role of women. Some have asked me if the Church, in fact, can even be classified as a Christian religion.

During my Miss America year, reporters questioned me on a daily basis about my religion—sometimes respectfully, but frequently with a lot of cynicism. Many of the questions were the same, but I tried to respond as though I had never been asked such a thoughtful, intelligent question before. Occasionally, someone would come up with a question I truly had never been asked, and when that happened I learned to rely heavily on the promptings of the Holy Ghost for an appropriate response. There was always a danger that I would say something that could be misunderstood or misinterpreted (I was especially worried that I might not be quoted correctly), and I didn't want to embarrass the Church—or myself, for that matter. Even though I stuck my foot in my mouth on occasion, I was grateful for the Lord's help, which made it possible to avoid any public relations disaster.

Prior to competing in the Miss America pageant, I spent a lot of time studying the moral issues facing both the Church and the nation. It was a sure thing that sooner or later I would be asked about the Church's stand on the Equal Rights Amendment (to the Constitution) or how I felt about abortion. And since I was from Utah, it was also a good bet I would be asked about polygamy. The Church Public Affairs Department was very helpful and provided me with information that clearly explained our stand on these and many other issues. What I especially appreciated were the thoughtful responses the Church had already prepared for addressing common doctrinal misconceptions. I also had the benefit of spending a few hours talking with Kathleen Lubeck in that department, and she helped me learn to communicate our beliefs in a way that was not likely to offend or be misinterpreted. I felt I was entering the media melee as prepared as possible. And that's the key right there, isn't it? "If ye are prepared ye shall not fear" (D&C 38:30).

However, before dealing with specific responses, here are

a few principles I discovered that helped me more effectively explain the gospel:

1. To quickly eliminate confusion, state as clearly and concisely as you can the Church's position on the topic in question.

2. Try not to overwhelm the person asking the question with too much information or doctrine. Instead, be prepared to give a short answer, unless, of course, the situation lends itself to a more detailed explanation. You'll need to rely on the Spirit to guide you. But, remember to offer simple answers, "milk before meat" (see 1 Corinthians 3:1–3; Hebrews 5:12–14).

3. Never sound hesitant or unsure. If you stammer around trying to formulate a diplomatic or "politically correct" reply, or hesitate because you are just guessing on the answer, the questioner will most certainly not be impressed with your response and may even be more critical of what you say. At the same time, though, be careful not to come across as overbearing and offensive.

4. Never dismiss a question as unimportant. Instead, use a little tact by saying, "You know, that's a very good question—and I believe I have an answer for you."

5. If you don't have an answer, say so. Just say, "I'll have to find out and get back with you on that." That approach shows you are confident in your beliefs and that there are answers available, without giving the impression you are a "Bible-bashing" know-it-all who is ready for any and all confrontations.

6. Instead of bristling at questions, field each one as though the questioner is honestly curious about our beliefs. Even if he or she seems belligerent, don't assume some sort of hostile intent on their part. Nothing useful will come of a confronta-

tion. A calm, kind, and dignified response is not going to pro-
voke any hard feelings or ill will, and any discussion where the
Holy Ghost can't be present isn't likely to do any good, anyway.

7. Use your sense of humor where appropriate. While you
should never make fun of the Church or its doctrines, there are
times when a little laughter can help create a feeling of goodwill. In other words, as Chieko Okazaki, former member of
the Relief Society general presidency, would say, "Lighten up!"
(See *Lighten Up!* [Salt Lake City: Deseret Book Company,
1993).

8. Be mindful of how you use LDS terminology to explain
our doctrines and beliefs. A classic example is casually refer-
ring to the "stake house"—naturally, your friend would
probably be expecting a thick, juicy steak upon arrival. I once
heard a sacrament meeting speaker share a humorous exchange
between his son and the son's friend. This brother had overheard his son and best friend talking about the temple. "What
happens in temple ceremonies?" the friend asked in a whisper.
The son replied, also in a whisper and with wide, anxious eyes,
"I don't know, but I heard they take out your endowments and
then seal you up!" To those unfamiliar with LDS terminology,
some words and phrases can sound bizarre. Choose words that
everyone would understand. For instance, instead of "in my
ward" (some people might immediately think of a hospital or
mental ward!), say "in my congregation."

In formulating the following ideas and responses, I would
like to thank Val Edwards of the Church's Public Affairs
Department, who provided me with invaluable assistance.
Maybe this information will help you respond more effectively

when a friend, a business associate, or even a stranger asks you an unexpected or off-the-wall question. I have organized this material into topics that are frequently addressed, beginning with how The Church of Jesus Christ of Latter-day Saints came into being.

THE ORIGIN OF OUR BELIEFS. The myths and misconceptions about the Church that continue to float around the world never cease to amaze me. I suppose I expect people to be more knowledgeable, but then, there are many things I don't know about the cultures and customs of the rest of the world. Keeping that in mind has allowed me to view some of the things I have been asked in a more charitable light. Many of the questions the world has about Mormonism really are the products of plain old curiosity. After all, the history of the Church and the events of the Restoration, while true, constitute a fantastic sequence of events that are to be accepted and understood only through the promptings of the Holy Ghost. The Prophet Joseph Smith, himself, said, "I don't blame any one for not believing my history. If I had not experienced what I have, I would not have believed it myself" (*History of the Church,* 6:317). There is no reason to be defensive nor, on the other hand, overly exuberant when someone asks about our first prophet, Joseph Smith, and how he organized this church. Most likely, they are just curious. Be helpful and informative in a kind, matter-of-fact way.

I recall one winter afternoon in New York City as my agent and I were hurrying to an interview. The sidewalks were crowded, cars were screeching and horns blaring, and the ever-present sounds of construction work were all effective in keeping our conversation down to a minimum. But even so, my agent (who is Jewish) took the opportunity to ask me how long I had been a Mormon. I told him (or rather, yelled back at him so he could hear me) that I had been born a member of the Church. He then asked how my church originated. At first I thought, "Great! He's interested in the Church!" But then, just as quickly, I realized he was simply curious. And given the environment we were in, it was hardly the time for a meaningful discussion where the Spirit would be welcome to testify of the truth. So I gave him just the facts: Joseph Smith, heightened religious interest in New England, the First Vision (1820), the things God the Father and Jesus Christ told him in the Sacred Grove, and subsequently, the translation of the Book of Mormon.

As I related this account, I got the impression that he had never heard such a fantastic story, and I could easily see the doubts written all over his face—concerning not only my story but my mental health as well. For an instant, I understood how Joseph felt when he said, "I don't blame any one for not believing my history" (*History of the Church* 6:317). Even *he* knew it was hard to believe! Yes, we will sometimes receive strange looks when we tell of how God the Father and his Son actually came in person to a fourteen-year-old boy in New York. But as you tell the story, don't allow embarrassment or fear of being considered a religious fanatic trip up your ability to speak confidently. The origin of our beliefs, even the wonder of the Restoration, is a very significant testimony to faithful Latter-day Saints, for everything we believe hinges on what took place in the Sacred Grove.

POLYGAMY. On my first day as an eighth grader at the American School in Buenos Aires, Argentina, I was already nervous about making friends when two thirteen-year-old classmates approached me. They said hi, and then in all seriousness, they asked when my horns might begin to grow out of my head. I could tell they weren't trying to make fun of me, they were just intensely interested in something that had been told to them. Still, I immediately felt that my chances of fitting in were pretty slim. After I had explained to them that none of the Mormons I knew had horns and that I had never heard of such a phenomenon, they accepted that and went on to their next question.

"How many mothers do you have?" they were eager to know.

I hated to disappoint them again with the truth but replied, "Just one." Again, I explained that I didn't know any Mormons who had more than one wife at the same time. That explanation seemed to satisfy them. I suppose the word quickly spread that I was as normal as any one of them, and no one ever asked me those kinds of questions at that school again.

The following is a recent statement on polygamy from the Public Affairs Department of the Church:

> The Church of Jesus Christ of Latter-day Saints declares that "marriage between a man and a woman is ordained of God and that the family is central to the Creator's plan for the eternal destiny of His children" ("The Family—A Proclamation to the World"). Although practiced by some Church members as a commandment from God during earlier times, polygamy has not been an authorized practice of the Church since 1890.
>
> • For several decades in the early history of the Church, polygamy was practiced among some members. Church

leaders endorsed such marriages in response to divine command. Those who practiced polygamy were called to do so by Church leaders.

- God has permitted or commanded polygamy at other times as evidenced by the lives of many Old Testament prophets.
- Members in polygamous marriages were bound by commitments to marital fidelity and Christlike living.
- After the United States government passed anti-polygamy laws, Church President Wilford Woodruff sought guidance from the Lord. In 1890, a revelation was received by President Woodruff declaring that polygamy was no longer authorized.
- Those already practicing plural marriage were not asked to abandon their wives and children. Once that transitional period had passed, however, the position of the Church was that no person could enter into a polygamous relationship and remain a member of the Church. That policy was adopted in general conference and has been reaffirmed by successive presidents of the Church.
- Groups and individuals practicing polygamy today have absolutely no connection to or affiliation with the Church of Jesus Christ of Latter-day Saints. (Public Affairs Department, The Church of Jesus Christ of Latter-day Saints)

Here are some suggested points to remember on the matter of polygamy:

1. The Church teaches that monogamous marriage is sacred and does not condone the practice of polygamy. Anyone who enters into polygamy is excommunicated from the Church, even if they live in a country where polygamy is legal or is an accepted cultural practice.

2. Under divine approval, some patriarchs of the Old Testament had more than one wife. The Church is founded upon the restoration of priesthood keys from all previous ages, and through revelation, early members of the Church in this dispensation were selectively instructed to practice polygamy.

3. We believe in upholding the laws of the land, so when the government passed anti-polygamy laws, our prophet went before the Lord and asked for direction. It was then (1890) that the Lord revealed that plural marriage was no longer an authorized practice.

THE ROLE OF AFRICAN-AMERICANS IN THE CHURCH. Not too long ago, while on an ESPN college football assignment in Iowa, I was in a restaurant with three of my colleagues the night before the game. The service was slow, which gave us a lot of time for conversation. Somehow the discussion turned to Utah and the fact that I am a Mormon. One of my dinner companions piped up and said, "Don't you believe that blacks did something wrong in a previous life and that's why they're black and aren't given the same responsibilities in your church?"

Either by divine intervention or pure luck, our waitress came at that moment with our food. All eyes were now on the steaming plates in front of them instead of on me, and it was apparent that a short reply would satisfy my friend's curiosity.

"Well, actually, they do have the same responsibilities in our church as anyone else," I began. "But I'm not too familiar with the other statement you made. I'll have to get back to you on that."

With their mouths full and the attention diverted, they nodded. I was relieved. *But,* I thought, *what if I'm asked about*

*that again, and there's no waitress around to save me? How should I
respond?*

Since then I've done some research—it's no fun to be
caught unprepared, looking like a deer caught in the headlights
of an approaching car—and I have an answer. If I were asked
that question now, I would, first of all, explain that today, *all*
worthy male members of the Church who are twelve years of
age or older are entitled to hold the priesthood. Period. Then I
might paraphrase the position of the Church on racial equality,
which was well articulated in a statement released by the
Church's Public Affairs Department:

> The concern of The Church of Jesus Christ of Latter-
> day Saints for the well-being and equality of all men and
> women was well defined by President Ezra Taft Benson as
> he began his present responsibilities:
>
> "My heart has been filled with an overwhelming love
> and compassion for all members of the Church and our
> Heavenly Father's children everywhere. I love all our
> Father's children of every color, creed, and political persua-
> sion." (*President Ezra Taft Benson, November 11, 1985.*) . . .
>
> "There is in this Church no doctrine, belief, or practice
> that is intended to deny the enjoyment of full civil rights by
> any person regardless of race, color, or creed. We call upon
> all men and women everywhere, both within and outside
> the Church, to commit themselves to the establishment of
> full civil equality for all of God's children. Anything less
> than this defeats our high ideal of the brotherhood of man."
> (*President Hugh B. Brown, General Conference, October 6, 1963.*)
>
> We repudiate efforts to deny to any person his or her
> inalienable dignity and rights on the abhorrent and tragic
> theory of the superiority of one race or color over another.

(Public Communications/Special Affairs Department, The Church of Jesus Christ of Latter-day Saints, 9 December 1987)

But it still remains to explain why the priesthood was for a time in our history withheld from black men. *Is* it our belief that they "did something wrong in a previous life"? While there might be some Church members who believe that, I have never read it in the scriptures nor heard General Authorities teach such a thing. In researching, I found nothing to support such a theory. In fact, I continually ran across writings that would suggest the complete opposite.

> Joseph Smith brushed aside all class lines, declaring in words of soberness that "God is no respecter of persons." Rich or poor, bond and free, learned and unlearned, male and female, meet and worship in common brotherhood and are judged by a common standard. While men and women are called to labor in different positions according to their several capacities and circumstances, neither birth nor social prominence nor money become a criterion for selection. (William Edwin Berrett, *The Restored Church,* 12th ed. [Salt Lake City: Deseret Book Company, 1961], p. 422)

During the 1960s and early 1970s, when racial matters in the United States were so much in the news, President Joseph Fielding Smith stated, "It is not the authorities of the Church who have placed a restriction on [the black] regarding the holding of the priesthood. It was not the Prophet Joseph Smith nor Brigham Young. It was the Lord!" (*Answers to Gospel Questions,* 5 vols., comp. Joseph Fielding Smith Jr. [Salt Lake City: Deseret Book Company, 1958], 2:185).

There have been many theories put forward, based on scriptural *interpretation,* but as far as I have been able to discover, we don't know *why* the blacks weren't able to hold the priesthood prior to 1978. The Doctine and Covenants statement, Official Declaration–2, mentions that "a revelation [was] received by President Spencer W. Kimball," but the declaration contains no explanation, saying simply that the time had arrived for "extending priesthood and temple blessings to all worthy male members of the Church." To speculate whether it had something to do with premortal circumstances or the social mores of the time or anything else is just that—speculation.

The letter written by the First Presidency in June 1978 and sent to all general and local priesthood officers of the Church throughout the world is a beautiful example of concentrating on present-day revelation and promises of the future, rather than dwelling on unknowns of the past. The letter declared:

> As we have witnessed the expansion of the work of the Lord over the earth, we have been grateful that people of many nations have responded to the message of the restored gospel, and have joined the Church in ever-increasing numbers. This, in turn, has inspired us with a desire to extend to every worthy member of the Church all of the privileges and blessings which the gospel affords.
>
> Aware of the promises made by the prophets and presidents of the Church who have preceded us that at some time, in God's eternal plan, all of our brethren who are worthy may receive the priesthood, and witnessing the faithfulness of those from whom the priesthood has been withheld, we have pleaded long and earnestly in behalf of these, our faithful brethren, spending many hours in the Upper Room of the Temple supplicating the Lord for divine guidance.

He has heard our prayers, and by revelation has confirmed that the long-promised day has come when every faithful, worthy man in the Church may receive the holy priesthood, with power to exercise its divine authority, and enjoy with his loved ones every blessing that flows therefrom, including the blessings of the temple. Accordingly, all worthy male members of the Church may be ordained to the priesthood without regard for race or color. (D&C Official Declaration—2)

I vividly recall one day in 1978. I was standing at the bottom of the stairs in our Buenos Aires home when my mother came out of her upstairs room with an excited shout. She came down the stairs and, with tears in her eyes yet a smile on her face, told me word had just come from Salt Lake City that the priesthood was to be extended to all worthy males. We hugged, and she told me she had waited all her life for that moment. Then she named many wonderful black members of the Church who had patiently lived the gospel without the priesthood in their homes. We were thrilled to think what the revelation would mean to them. The 1978 declaration is yet another reminder that the Lord's Church is guided by continuing revelation.

Suggested points to remember include the following:

1. Today, all worthy male members of the Church are entitled to hold the priesthood.

2. Just as we don't know why Jesus Christ initially withheld the gospel from the Gentiles until after his death and resurrection, we likewise haven't been told why the priesthood was withheld from the blacks until 1978.

THE ROLE OF WOMEN IN THE CHURCH. One question I have frequently been asked has to do with the role of women in the Church. I was surprised to discover that many people mistakenly view us as a backward and repressive society where female members of the Church all wear their hair in buns and spend time hand-churning butter.

At first, I thought reporters were joking when they asked about "the sorry state of women in the Mormon church" or when they suggested that women were less favored than men in our religion. It had never occurred to me that Mormon women might be subjugated or thought of as inferior to men. (Well, except for a time when I was fourteen, and I wondered why young men were allowed to go on missions at nineteen while young women had to wait until they turned twenty-one. For someone anxious to serve a mission, it seemed as though the boys were receiving preferential treatment! But I hardly viewed that as an indication that Mormon women were in a "sorry state.")

In one of my press conferences, one female reporter asked, "Aren't women second-class citizens in your church, and isn't that why women don't occupy any leadership positions?"

Whenever I was confronted with that kind of statement, I usually referred to something I had heard Marie Osmond once say. This is not a direct quote, but Marie essentially said that women are equal to men in the Church, but we aren't the *same*. We believe in *equality* but not in *sameness*.

It used to irritate me when people implied that women occupy some inferior station in the Church, and I learned to be pretty blunt in response to that kind of assumption—partly because I had never been made to feel as though I were an inferior member of the Church because I was a woman, and partly because it's so obvious to me that women *do* play an important role in the Church.

Utah was the first state to give women the right to vote. The Relief Society, which was organized in 1842, is the largest and oldest women's organization in the world and is directed by women. Our women serve as missionaries, preach sermons from the pulpit in worship services, lead congregational prayers, hold administrative and teaching positions at all levels, and serve in the Church's governing auxiliary councils.

Aside from all that, I have always appreciated the Church's emphasis on the differing roles played by men and women. Instead of trying to blur the lines and create what I refer to as a "neutered society," the Church has always emphasized the special places occupied by women and valued us for our unique characteristics and instincts. Take those attributes away from women, and it seems to me that our value would be diminished in many ways.

After making some of these points, I seldom had to field any follow-up questions on that subject. I recall feeling just a bit irritated whenever a reporter would infer that because I didn't hold the priesthood, I was somehow an inferior member of the Church. I used to wish these folks could spend just one day with my family. Then they would know how equal women are—in the Church and at home. I have always viewed my mom and dad as equal partners in their marriage and in our family. They each play a different role, but the roles are equally important. I grew up never questioning that relationship.

Now that I have had the beautiful experience of giving birth and being a mother, I clearly see that if anyone suffers from inequality in the gospel plan, it just might be the men, who have been denied that sacred privilege!

The Church's Public Affairs Department has issued this clear statement regarding women and the priesthood:

> The priesthood is defined as the authority given to man to act in the name of God. It is always described in the scriptures as coming through the lineage of the fathers (see Numbers 18:7; Joshua 18:7).
>
> All faithful and worthy Latter-day Saint men may be ordained to the priesthood. President Boyd K. Packer, acting president of the Quorum of the Twelve Apostles, has said, "From the beginning, the priesthood has been conferred only upon the men. The priesthood is not ours to remodel or change or modify or abridge. It is ours to honor and to magnify" (Priesthood Restoration Fireside, May 7, 1989).
>
> In the Church, those who have the priesthood are not viewed as being superior to those who do not. The priesthood is held upon a sacred obligation to use it to bless the lives of others.
>
> The priesthood, when understood and righteously exercised, unites men and women; it should never separate them. The highest eternal rewards the Lord bestows upon his children cannot be achieved by either man or woman alone. Such post-mortal rewards are accessible only to the worthy bearer of the priesthood and his equally worthy wife, who shares with him the blessings of that sacred authority. (Public Affairs Department, The Church of Jesus Christ of Latter-day Saints)

Remember the following points when discussing women and their role:

1. Men and women are equal but not the same. We believe in *equality,* not in *sameness.*

2. The Church's organization for women (the Relief Society) is the oldest and largest women's group in the world, directed by women. Women serve in the Church as missionaries, lead congregations in prayer, preach, teach, and administer on many levels. Women hold leadership positions in the auxiliary organizations—Primary, Young Women, and Relief Society.

3. The priesthood unites men and women; it should never separate them.

MORALITY. I would guess that in at least 95 percent of the press conferences and interviews I gave during my year as Miss America, questions were raised concerning my stand on morality. I had always been aware that the moral code taught by the Church was generally viewed by the world as outdated and old-fashioned, but I didn't realize just how peculiar we are thought to be because of it. Many people found it difficult, if not impossible, to believe that a twenty-year-old in today's society could hold such strict views on the importance of remaining virtuous in preparation for the sacred vows of marriage.

As you might imagine, I was anxious to prove myself an acceptable representative of American young women. I wanted to have my accomplishments recognized, deemed credible enough for such a role. And yet, I admit, I wanted to be accepted as a sophisticated "woman of the 80s."

But all anyone seemed to focus on was how anachronistic and out of touch with reality I was. I quickly became accustomed to the incredulous looks I would get whenever I responded to a question on morality. I wasn't ashamed of my beliefs by any means, but I grew to dislike the "you can't be serious" looks I would have to confront after explaining my stand. It wasn't much fun being treated like the star attraction in a freak show.

But I got used to it. And I became bolder and bolder in defending my position. I even got to the point where the "goody-goody" headlines that followed me everywhere in the local newspapers didn't bother me. I simply reminded myself of what the papers might be saying about me if I weren't so "goody-goody" and if I *did* have some skeletons in the closet. I decided to stop feeling like I was being picked on, and, instead, to represent myself as though I were the normal one in an abnormal world.

One of my first assignments with ESPN was to cover the World Cup Alpine Championships in Vail, Colorado. I had been working with a crew of four all day, gathering interviews and doing some on-camera segments. By dinnertime, we were all tired and hungry. We stopped to eat on the way back to headquarters, and after placing our orders, we relaxed, chatted, and watched the snow falling outside the window of the restaurant. Suddenly, one of the guys said to me, "You're a Mormon, right? Why are you so adamant about waiting until marriage—I mean, what's the big deal?"

I was the only female in the group, and I instantly became uncomfortable. His tone was mocking, and I felt his question was inappropriate. But before I could respond, the other three guys immediately cornered him, saying *they* were offended by what he had said. My producer said to him, "Come on. Do you know of any religion that *advocates* sexual relations before marriage? Show some respect and intelligence." Needless to say, the crew member was embarrassed and apologetic.

I have encountered all kinds of reactions to my beliefs on

morality, from disbelief to amusement, cynicism to support. Mostly, I have found that people admire us for the self-discipline we try to maintain and for our view that procreation is a sacred matter. For many, ours is a strict code, one that seems too stringent to be widely followed. But our stand on morality was not invented by man for the purpose of enslaving us. It originated with the Lord and is designed to liberate us.

President Gordon B. Hinckley read the following statement at the general Relief Society meeting held September 23, 1995. In this official declaration, titled "The Family: A Proclamation to the World," the First Presidency and Council of the Twelve Apostles clearly state the principles by which we are guided as a church:

> We, the First Presidency and the Council of the Twelve Apostles of The Church of Jesus Christ of Latter-day Saints, solemnly proclaim that marriage between a man and a woman is ordained of God and that the family is central to the Creator's plan for the eternal destiny of His children. . . . We further declare that God has commanded that the sacred powers of procreation are to be employed only between man and woman, lawfully wedded as husband and wife.
>
> We declare the means by which mortal life is created to be divinely appointed. We affirm the sanctity of life and of its importance in God's eternal plan. . . . Children are entitled to birth within the bonds of matrimony, and to be reared by a father and a mother who honor marital vows with complete fidelity. . . .
>
> We warn that individuals who violate covenants of chastity . . . will one day stand accountable before God.

And in a letter from the First Presidency to all priesthood leaders (14 November 1991), the following definition of moral conduct appeared: "The Lord's law of moral conduct is abstinence outside of lawful marriage and fidelity within marriage. Sexual relations are proper only between husband and wife, appropriately expressed within the bonds of marriage. Any other sexual contact, including fornication, adultery, and homosexual and lesbian behavior, is sinful. Those who persist in such practices or who influence others to do so are subject to Church discipline."

So there we have it: clear statements of where the Church stands on this issue. Church members can easily understand these principles, and if called upon, we should be able to explain our moral code to others.

The following are some points to remember when discussing the topic of sexual morality:

1. God's children have always been expected to observe strict codes of moral behavior, and all who claim to believe in God should have no reason to question that standard.

2. As Latter-day Saints, we consider marriage vows to be sacred. Therefore, even though we have the same natural desires as anyone else, we choose to practice self-discipline, not only out of loyalty to God, but to show loyalty to our intended spouse. Following marriage, there is no justification for unfaithful behavior.

3. Abstinence from illicit sexual experiences begets freedom—freedom from guilt, freedom from regret, freedom from disease.

WOMEN'S RIGHTS. Most friends and even casual acquaintances try to steer clear of hot political topics in their conversations. Discussing such issues as abortion, prayer in the classroom and in public meetings, and the Equal Rights

Amendment generally serves only to generate disagreement and get people who are normally friendly to become angry with each other.

But there may be times when your viewpoint will be solicited. It could be anywhere—in an airport, at a board meeting, in the classroom, or at a luncheon. It is important to have an informed opinion because if you don't, you become easy prey for those who have developed a point of view.

In the mid-1980s, the Equal Rights Amendment (often referred to as the ERA) was an emotionally charged topic. After the ERA was more or less laid to rest, the issues surrounding it didn't come up as frequently. But I was often asked my opinion about it in my news conferences and appearances during my year as Miss America. Because the debate goes right to the heart of the role of women in life and in the Church, this is something that should still be of concern to members of the Church; therefore, I would like to discuss it here.

The issues involved in that debate were gender issues, and they had a lot to do with the role women properly ought to play in society. From my point of view, the ERA debate was almost a religious debate. I knew how strongly the leaders of the Church felt about the matter, and I didn't want to inadvertently misrepresent the Church's position. It was important that I represent that stand accurately, and in attempting to do so, I may sometimes have come across as perhaps *too* dogmatic and somewhat narrow-minded. But I didn't want anyone to misunderstand my position, and I didn't want to leave myself open to criticism because of my being unclear.

The fact is that if the drive to pass the ERA had succeeded, and if women had been granted "equal rights," we women would have lost a great deal. It was clear to our Church leaders (and I agreed) that, rather than gaining rights and privileges, women would have lost many advantages and been made to assume many traditional male responsibilities, such as submitting to the military draft. The law would likely have been interpreted in such a way as to take away any special consideration for such things as pregnancy or family responsibilities—a truly frightening prospect and something that would have been detrimental to society.

The Church doesn't often take a public position on political issues, except in matters of morality, but it did come out in opposition to the ERA and to two other hotly debated topics. One is abortion, the other is banning prayer in public settings.

ABORTION. The topic of abortion is a volatile one for many Americans, and the seemingly endless discussions have turned the debate into a virtual civil war. I was asked so often about my stand on this issue that I developed a response that was almost memorized. I basically said the following:

"I believe in individual free agency, *and* I believe in a human being's right to life. I hold both principles to be sacred. But when the two conflict (as they do when a woman tries to decide whether or not to have an abortion), there is no doubt in my mind which principle has priority: I stand for the right to life. At that point, the woman needs to surrender her agency in the interest of the unborn child. An analogy would be that of a stop sign. We may have the freedom to ignore the signal, but we do so at the peril of our safety and that of others. We therefore surrender the freedom to go through the stop sign, in the interest of a higher good. Rare circumstances where abortion may be considered are when the pregnancy is the result of rape or incest, or when the pregnancy puts the life of the mother in danger. Next question?" I tried to keep my answer simple to make it easier for the reporters to quote me accurately.

In January 1991, the Church issued an official statement on abortion that leaves no doubt what our position ought to be:

> In view of the widespread public interest in the issue of abortion, we reaffirm that The Church of Jesus Christ of Latter-day Saints has consistently opposed elective abortion. More than a century ago, the First Presidency of the Church warned against this evil. We have repeatedly counseled people everywhere to turn from the devastating practice of abortion for personal or social convenience.
>
> The Church recognizes that there may be rare cases in which abortion may be justified—cases involving pregnancy by incest or rape; when the life or health of the woman is adjudged by competent medical authority to be in serious jeopardy; or when the fetus is known by competent medical authority to have severe defects that will not allow the baby to survive beyond birth. But these are not automatic reasons for abortion. Even in these cases, the couple should consider an abortion only after consulting with each other, and their bishop, and receiving divine confirmation through prayer.
>
> The practice of elective abortion is fundamentally contrary to the Lord's injunction, "Thou shalt not steal; neither commit adultery, nor kill, nor do anything like unto it." (D&C 59:6.) We urge all to preserve the sanctity of human life and thereby realize the happiness promised to those who keep the commandments of the Lord.
>
> The Church of Jesus Christ of Latter-day Saints as an institution has not favored or opposed specific legislative proposals or public demonstrations concerning abortion.
>
> Inasmuch as this issue is likely to arise in all states in the

United States of America and in many other nations of the world in which the Church is established, it is impractical for the Church to take a position on specific legislative proposals on this important subject.

However, we continue to encourage our members as citizens to let their voices be heard in appropriate and legal ways that will evidence their belief in the sacredness of life. ("Statement issued on abortion," *Church News,* 19 January 1991, p. 5)

One year after giving up his practice as an internationally known heart surgeon to accept a calling to become a member of the Quorum of the Twelve Apostles, Elder Russell M. Nelson gave a comprehensive talk on this subject in general conference. Among other things, he pointed out that abortion claims more lives annually than the total number—more than a million— of the lives lost in all the wars the United States has fought in its history.

He quoted sixteenth-century reformer John Calvin, who wrote, "If it seems more horrible to kill a man in his own house than in a field—since for every man his home is his sanctuary— how much more abominable it is . . . to kill a fetus . . . who has not yet been brought into the light."

He pointed out that the health of the mother is a proper concern in pregnancy, as is pregnancy resulting from rape or incest. But he also noted that "less than 3 percent of all abortions are performed for these two reasons. The other 97 percent are for what may be termed 'reasons of convenience.'"

"Some argue abortion because a malformed child may result. . . . If one is to be deprived of life because of potential for developing physical problems, consistency would dictate that those who already have such deficiencies should likewise be terminated. . . . Such irreverence for life is unthinkable!"

Elder Nelson said some may justify abortion by saying that a woman is free to choose what she does with her own body. That's true only to a certain extent, he pointed out: We are free to think, to plan, and to do. But once we have taken an action, we are never free from its consequences. Those considering abortion have already exercised some choices.

Elder Nelson used the analogy of an astronaut, who is free to withdraw his commitment to ride on the spaceship during the selection process, the planning, and the preparation for a flight. But once the rocket fuel is ignited, he no longer has freedom of choice. The same holds true for the woman who has made the decisions that have resulted in pregnancy. She has the freedom to choose her course of action up until the time of conception. Then she no longer is free to choose. Elder Nelson continued:

> The consequence of terminating the fetus therein involves the body and very life of another. These two individuals have separate brains, separate hearts, and separate circulatory systems. To pretend that there is no child and no life there is to deny reality. . . .
>
> In biological sciences, it is known that life begins when two germ cells unite to become one cell, bringing together twenty-three chromosomes from both the father and from the mother. . . .
>
> The onset of life is not a debatable issue but a fact of science. . . .
>
> Approximately twenty-two days after the two cells have united, a little heart begins to beat. At twenty-six days the circulation of blood begins.
>
> Life . . . is a gift from our Heavenly Father. It is eternal,

as he is eternal. Innocent life is not sent by him to be destroyed! ("Reverence for Life," *Ensign,* May 1985, pp. 11–14)

Here are some points to remember regarding abortion:

1. Freedom of choice and the right to life are two vital human rights. But when the two conflict, the right to life takes precedence.

2. Abortion may be justified only in the case of rape, incest, or when the life of the mother is in danger or when competent medical opinion holds that the fetus will not survive beyond birth. Even then, abortion should only be considered after the parents have consulted with each other and with the Lord.

3. The freedom to choose is void once pregnancy has resulted. We are all subject to the consequences of our acts.

4. The woman's right to choose doesn't extend beyond her own body. She and the fetus are two separate individuals. The mother's responsibility is to provide a safe, healthy environment for the baby to develop and grow.

PUBLIC PRAYER. Another issue I was frequently asked about is the politically "hot" topic of public prayer. I recall having to respond occasionally to questions about the Church's stand on whether or not prayer should be allowed in the classrooms of our public schools. (At the time the debate had not been extended to include prayer in public meetings.) When asked, I generally said that our Founding Fathers established this nation to secure for its citizens certain basic freedoms, among them freedom of religion. Not only that, but those same Founding Fathers openly demonstrated their devotion to God and their dependence on him through prayer. Their commitment to religion is evidenced by the phrase "In God We Trust," which has always been part of the design of U.S. coins and paper money. It seems evident to me that a belief in God is one of the basic principles on which our nation is anchored. In my opinion, we demean the very existence of the United States of America by not allowing its citizens to pray how and when we choose—in public or in private. But as a church we must follow legal guidelines until they can be changed.

The following statement was published in the *Church News* on 27 October 1990:

> The Church of Jesus Christ of Latter-day Saints has always emphasized the importance of prayer, including prayers offered in any public setting in which they are legal.
>
> The Supreme Court of the United States has clearly forbidden any audible prayers in public school classrooms. We encourage all to observe that ruling.
>
> The constitutionality of prayers in public school graduations and other high school events is still before the courts in a variety of cases of differing circumstances. This is a national issue. We welcome the opportunity for duly constituted authorities to examine the educational practices and religious traditions of the nation and to clarify the law on this important subject. [Since this statement was issued, the Supreme Court has ruled (in 1992) that school officials who arrange for a prayer to be said as a part of an official public school graduation ceremony imply their endorsement of religion and thereby violate the principle of the separation of church and state.]
>
> Where prayer is legally permissible . . . we believe no one should be required to modify the content of the prayer he or she chooses to offer regardless of religious affiliation.

Prayer is too sacred for its content to be the subject of a lawsuit.

In discussion of these issues, we need goodwill and considerate behavior on the part of all.

As the ruling principle of conduct in the lives of many millions of our citizens, religion should have an honorable place in the public life of our nation, and the name of Almighty God should have sacred use in its public expressions. ("Statement expresses position on prayer," *Church News*, 27 October 1990, p. 4)

The following are several points to remember with regard to public prayers:

1. We emphasize the importance of prayer but declare our intention to observe U.S. Supreme Court rulings regarding public prayer.

2. Where prayer is legally permissible, we believe no one should be required to modify the content of the prayer he or she chooses to offer, regardless of religion.

3. The motto of the United States of America is "In God We Trust." If that is to mean anything, then prayer ought to be a natural and common occurrence in our everyday lives. Surely, the banning of public prayers serves to mock this motto.

These are just a sampling of the sensitive issues members of the Church might be asked to address, and a fairly broad sampling at that. The answers I have offered may not be the best, and they're certainly not the only way to word replies. I encourage you to prepare for anything by first imagining situations in which you might be asked delicate questions and then thinking about what you might say. As members of the Church, we need to be prepared to explain or defend what we believe if we are to be "beacons" to those who have lost their way or who are looking for the truth. In the next chapter, I'll continue to look at some of the questions I have encountered over the years, many I'm sure you have likewise come across.

ANSWERS TO COMMONLY ASKED GOSPEL QUESTIONS

Y ou never know where you'll meet someone who will ask a provocative question about the Church or our beliefs. Just two weeks after our honeymoon, my husband, Bob, and I went to London, where we had been invited by the Church to participate in the sesquicentennial celebration of the presence of the Church in the British Isles. Naturally, we were honored to be invited and excited to contribute in any way we could to the building of good public relations. We had an opportunity to speak at firesides and to give a few interviews. One interview took place on a popular morning TV show in Britain, comparable to our *Good Morning, America*. It turned into a memorable experience.

Having been asked just about every imaginable question during my several years of experience with the press, I had no reason to believe that this interview would involve anything I hadn't handled before. Still, I was nervous and wanted to do well. I offered a silent prayer, asking Heavenly Father to help me answer any Church-related questions. Since I was well aware of my tendency to be a little defensive, I promised the Lord that I would try to curb that tendency and trust the promptings of the Spirit.

The interviewer asked me about the missionary program and about our policy on dating and abstinence from sexual relations before marriage—questions I had responded to many times before. Overall, it was a very pleasant experience, until her last question.

"I understand," she began with a smile on her face, "that you Mormons like to collect names of dead people, and that you go from cemetery to cemetery writing them all down!" Then with a cynical laugh and a glance at her cohost, she added, "That sounds rather sinister to me!" She and her partner both stared at me, and I was very much on the spot to respond.

My answer was brief and quite simple. It was near the end of the show, and before I could say very much, the show's theme music began to play, which was my cue to be quiet and the hosts' cue to interrupt me. About all I had time to say was that the practice of collecting the names of our ancestors is not sinister at all, that the researching of genealogies is a common practice, even among people of other faiths, but that we do so in a belief that families can continue in the eternities. After the show, she apologized for putting me on the spot like that but explained that it was her job to ask provocative questions.

FAMILY HISTORY. Most people, when they learn of our interest in genealogical research, are not confused by the practice. Instead, their questions deal more with our temple work and, specifically, why we perform baptisms for the dead. Some people are baffled because they have the impression we *literally* baptize the dead, rather than perform proxy ordinances. (That *does* sound sinister!)

Here is what the Church's media guide says on this subject:

For millions of people who lived before the time of Christ or during the intervening centuries between the death of the Apostles and the Restoration of his Church, temple and other vital ordinances were not available. Even today, millions live and die without ever hearing the name of Jesus Christ or without learning the saving principles and accepting the ordinances of the gospel he taught.

Provision must be made, then, for those who have died without that opportunity. The Church of Jesus Christ of Latter-day Saints teaches that all saving ordinances are to be performed on earth in behalf of the dead. Latter-day Saints stand as proxies for their own ancestors in these cere-monies, including baptisms and sealings for husbands and wives and parents and children. All temple work is valid only if it is willingly accepted by each individual prior to the resurrection.

Performing temple ordinances receives strong emphasis in the Church. Members are taught that they have a reli-gious obligation to trace their own genealogies and perform temple ordinances for their ancestors. (*Global Media Guide* [Salt Lake City: The Church of Jesus Christ of Latter-day Saints])

Our understanding that our departed ancestors have not ceased to exist but have instead moved into another sphere of life, where they're very much "alive," makes the practice of proxy work in their behalf more comprehensible.

Points to remember include the following:

1. We believe that families are eternal units, and genealogy work helps us identify and learn about our ancestors.

2. Most Christian religions accept baptism as a prerequisite for entering the kingdom of heaven. Through genealogical

research, we are able to locate ancestors who have not had the benefit of the ordinances of baptism or of eternal marriage.

3. In the temples we perform these ordinances, by proxy, for these individuals. They retain their agency and have the option of accepting or rejecting the work done on their behalf.

4. This revealed doctrine shows the Lord's fairness. While he requires all of us to submit to certain ordinances in order to be "saved," he has provided a way that doesn't exclude anyone from having an opportunity to receive the necessary ordinances. It is a glorious plan.

5. "Baptism for the dead" is a practice Saints in the New Testament were familiar with, as evidenced by Paul's reference to it. In an attempt to persuade his readers that the Resurrection is literal, he reasoned, "Else what shall they do which are baptized for the dead, if the dead rise not at all? why are they then baptized for the dead?" (1 Corinthians 15:29).

ARE MORMONS CHRISTIANS? Recently, the national media picked up on a story of a young man who belonged to the Fellowship of Christian Athletes. Although his school nominated him to receive the FCA's top honor, the state FCA denied him the award because he is Mormon and not a Christian. Fortunately, the media acted responsibly in this case and reported the facts, which supported The Church of Jesus Christ of Latter-day Saints as indeed a Christian faith!

An impression has somehow been created in the world that Mormons are not Christians. Mormonism is occasionally even said to be a *cult*. Webster's dictionary defines a cult as "a religion regarded as unorthodox or spurious" that is characterized as growing out of "great devotion to a person, idea, object, movement, or work."

Those who accuse us of being a cult may mistakenly assume that we worship Joseph Smith or erroneously believe we are devoted to a "golden Bible."

The truth is that the central figure of our faith is the Lord Jesus Christ, whom we revere as our Savior, Redeemer, and the literal Son of God, the Eternal Father. Members of the Church testify that Jesus Christ lived, died, and was resurrected for our sake. Even the name of our church—The Church of Jesus Christ of Latter-day Saints—reflects our belief in him. He is central to our doctrines, and without his atoning sacrifice, we know we have no hope of redemption from sin.

When we lived in South America, my dad had an experience that shows how we are frequently misunderstood. He was traveling on an airplane and was seated next to a sophisticated international engineer who spoke many languages and had traveled widely. Their conversation turned to religion, and the man commented, "You Mormons have surely built a magnificent shrine at Joseph Smith's gravesite."

In surprise, Dad exclaimed, "What shrine? What gravesite?"

"Why, that tall building in Salt Lake City with the gold angel on top. Isn't that a mausoleum or shrine of some kind where you worship your prophet?"

Dad was happy to have the opportunity to help the man understand more accurately who we are and what we believe. He explained that Mormons are most definitely Christians and that we worship only God the Father in the name of his Son, Jesus Christ. He emphasized that we do *not* worship the Prophet Joseph Smith, and that though we honor and love him, we never pray to him or kneel in front of statues of him. Dad also explained that in our doctrines, philosophy, and practices,

Joseph Smith is not an intermediary of any kind. Christ alone is our advocate with the Father.

To correct his traveling companion's other misconception, Dad explained that the temple in Salt Lake City was not built to honor Joseph Smith and that he isn't even buried there. Dad said to him, "Please believe me when I say that we never make a pilgrimage to where the Prophet Joseph is buried." Many Latter-day Saint families visit Church historical sites, of course, but they do so because of their love of the gospel and of history, not because it is in any way a prescribed religious duty.

When people ask if we are a cult or if we are Christians, we must answer them directly and to the point. We will often have only a minute or two to respond, and we ought to use that time to declare in no uncertain terms who it is that we follow and revere—Jesus of Nazareth, who is the Only Begotten of the Father in the flesh, the resurrected Lord. It is hard to imagine a statement of belief more powerful on this subject than the one Nephi made in the Book of Mormon: "We talk of Christ, we rejoice in Christ, we preach of Christ, we prophesy of Christ, and we write according to our prophecies, that our children may know to what source they may look for a remission of their sins" (2 Nephi 25:26). It would be wise to memorize this passage.

WHAT DO MORMONS BELIEVE? In the past twelve years as I have flown to the various events assigned to me in my sportscasting work, I have often found myself wandering the busy but lonely waiting areas of airports. Most of the time I had very close connections to make, but one time during my last season, I had a disappointing three-hour layover in Atlanta on my way home.

I made my way over to a food court and decided on a plate of Chinese food for my dinner. As I sat there eating, I pulled out my family pictures and stared at them awhile. A man who was seated nearby noticed my pictures and commented that he too had a family waiting for him at home and that he had been stuck in Atlanta for four hours. We began to talk about our families and the reasons we were away from them. He was an international businessman of some sort.

After about twenty minutes, two of my ESPN colleagues happened by and joined us at our table. We made introductions, and it somehow came up that I was a Mormon. The two who had joined us got up to buy some food and drinks, and as they left, my new friend immediately said, "I have to leave in five minutes, but I'd like to know, what do Mormons believe?"

The first thing I thought was, *Where do I start?* What could I say about what we believe, in five minutes or less? I wanted to make a clear, easy-to-understand statement. You may have to do the same thing. When you are walking down a busy downtown sidewalk, with horns blaring, people yelling and jostling, and construction equipment operating, a co-worker or friend suddenly asks, "So, what do Mormons believe?" as my agent did in New York one day (see pp. 124–25). What will you say? If you can do so, it would be best to ask your friend to wait until you get to a more peaceful environment before trying to answer. But what if it's a person you're not likely to ever see again?

Don't try to lay out *everything* for review—there is simply too much information for anyone to digest. You might be tempted to frantically recite the Articles of Faith that you memorized in Primary, but comprehensive as they are, they're not very conversational in their written form. Here's how I answer that question, and it may work for you, too. Tell your friend you can lend him volumes of books on what we believe, but for simplicity's sake, you can offer him three main beliefs to initially consider:

1. Mormons are Christians. Christ is the cornerstone of the church that bears his name—The Church of Jesus Christ of Latter-day Saints. We teach of Christ, we preach of Christ, and we believe salvation comes only in and through his sacred name. We believe he is the literal Son of God the eternal Father. At this point you might also indicate our belief in three separate members of the Godhead; in other words, share the first Article of Faith: "We believe in God, the Eternal Father, and in His Son, Jesus Christ, and in the Holy Ghost."

2. We believe not only in the Holy Bible but also in a book called the Book of Mormon, which is the keystone of our religion. Just as the prophets of God lived in the Eastern Hemisphere and recorded revelations and religious history, God had ancient prophets that lived in the Western Hemisphere who did the same. These writings are contained in the Book of Mormon (see Articles of Faith 1:8).

3. We believe that just as the Lord spoke to his ancient servants—prophets such as Noah, Abraham, and Moses—so he speaks today through modern prophets, beginning with Joseph Smith and continuing down to President Gordon B. Hinckley. Through these modern prophets, the Lord has restored his church and gospel to the earth.

THE BOOK OF MORMON. As a further way of introducing the Book of Mormon, I have found it useful to do something like this: Explain that the Book of Mormon is an ancient record that contains the history of the people who lived on the American continent, to whom Christ paid a visit after his resurrection. In John 10:16, Jesus made a clear statement that he had "other sheep," who were destined to also hear his voice. He in fact appeared to them, and the Book of Mormon contains a record of the things he said and did at that time.

Some people find it interesting to learn that the first European explorers to encounter Native Americans were often very nearly worshipped by those they eventually conquered. The Aztecs, for instance, didn't resist Cortez, thinking him to be the legendary "bearded white man [who] appeared long ago, taught a demanding set of spiritual principles, then departed mysteriously with the promise that he would return someday" (John L. Sorenson, *An Ancient American Setting for the Book of Mormon* [Salt Lake City: Deseret Book Company and F.A.R.M.S., 1996], p. 326). This was Quetzalcoatl, the supreme being that the Aztecs worshipped as the god of death and resurrection and revered as the god of Venus, or the Morning Star.

Because the account of the Savior's visit and teachings in the Americas are found in the Book of Mormon, it is called "Another Testament of Jesus Christ," and as such the book is a *companion* volume to the Bible, not a replacement for it. It came forth through the Prophet Joseph Smith, with whom the angel Moroni entrusted the gold plates on which the ancient record was inscribed. Joseph translated the ancient record "by the gift and power of God" for our benefit. Who wouldn't be interested in at least taking a look at a book that makes such claims as to its origin?

Do You Mormons Really Believe You Will Someday Be Gods? This is a particularly difficult question to answer because to someone who knows nothing of our beliefs, it sounds like such an arrogant thing to say.

Most people in the world today have only a vague understanding of who or what God is. For instance, when I was a sophomore in high school, I was sitting in my social science class one day when my teacher said something about the nature of God that really bothered me. In her discussion of the religion of a particular culture we were studying, she casually remarked that everyone knows that God is intangible, everywhere but nowhere in particular, and that he has no definable shape and can assume any form he wishes, etc., etc.

I was hesitant to openly challenge her. She was a brilliant woman who spoke eight languages fluently, held a law degree, had held important positions at the United Nations, and had opted to move back to her home in Argentina and take a teaching position at a private school. Nevertheless, I felt it was important to point out that not everyone shared her view of God.

I raised my hand, and when she called on me, I said I had a different concept of who God is. A bit startled, she asked me what it was. I responded by saying that I believe he *is* a tangible being with a body of flesh and bones, and that he is only omnipresent in the sense that his *influence* can be felt everywhere. She laughed at me and ridiculed what I had said, suggesting that it was naive to think of God as having a physical body.

It wasn't like me to talk back to my superiors, but she made me angry, and as eloquently as I could as a fifteen-year-old, I responded (as best I can recall), "I believe he does have a body, and it makes perfect sense to me that he would. I mean, when it says in the scriptures that God *sits* on his throne and that Christ will sit on the right *hand* of God—well, nebulous blobs don't sit, and they don't have hands. Bodies do. I say he has a body!"

Of course, the whole class just sat there and stared at me. To her credit, my teacher ended up conceding I had a right to my opinion, and she apologized for making fun of me.

That experience in school made me think more deeply about what I really believed. I had always been taught to pray, and when I did so I always imagined an exalted being who listened to my words—a being who was loving and fatherly. One who was listening sympathetically to my concerns and requests—someone a lot like my own dad. I found it impossible to think of worshipping or praying to or giving thanks to some undefined, vague spiritual presence.

Joseph Smith, who had actually seen God the Father and Jesus Christ, described the Godhead this way: "The Father has a body of flesh and bones as tangible as man's; the Son also; but the Holy Ghost has not a body of flesh and bones" (D&C 130:22). In another place the Prophet said, "I have always declared God to be a distinct personage, Jesus Christ a separate and distinct personage from God the Father, and that the Holy Ghost was a distinct personage and a Spirit: and these three constitute three distinct personages and three Gods" (*Teachings of the Prophet Joseph Smith* [Salt Lake City: Deseret News Press, 1938], p. 370).

Another quote from the Prophet details what he had learned through revelation about the nature of God:

> *God himself was once as we are now, and is an exalted man, and sits enthroned in yonder heavens! That is the great secret. If the*

veil were rent today, and the great God who holds this world in its orbit, and who upholds all worlds and all things by his power, was to make himself visible,—I say, if you were to see him today, you would see Him like a man in form—like yourselves in all the person, image, and very form as a man; for Adam was created in the very fashion, image and likeness of God, and received instruction from, and walked, talked and conversed with him, as one man talks and communes with another. (Ibid., p. 345)

It is a touchy thing to talk about differences in religion, and especially about something as intensely personal as one's belief in God. But even if someone has been trained in a religion that formally teaches (as many do) that God is intangible, that he is large enough to fill the universe, yet small enough to dwell in your heart, and so on, that person may not have really embraced such a vague concept. And if you can find a way to describe the way *you* envision Heavenly Father, it's quite possible that they will *feel* the same way. After all, members of most churches are comfortable calling him "Father."

Having established that much, you might ask your friend to think about *why* we call him "Father." The reason is that we are his spiritually begotten children, and the New Testament confirms that truth. Paul said, "The Spirit itself beareth witness with our spirit, that we are the children of God" (Romans 8:16).

Furthermore, the Bible says, "And God said, Let us make man in our image, after our likeness: . . . So God created man in his own image, in the image of God created he him; male and female created he them" (Genesis 1:26–27) It is hard to imagine anyone misunderstanding this statement. Even so, some people have asserted that this scripture doesn't mean Adam was created in the *physical* image and likeness of God. If that isn't what the scripture means, how do you explain what it says a chapter or two later: "And Adam . . . begat a son in his own likeness, after his image; and called his name Seth" (Genesis 5:3)? Didn't Seth resemble Adam? And, if so, didn't Adam resemble God?

From here it is not a great leap of logic to suggest that if we are God's children, and we resemble him physically, why can't we eventually become like him? Very simply, a puppy grows up to be a dog, a kitten grows up to be a cat. Teaching this doctrine, Elder Boyd K. Packer of the Quorum of the Twelve said:

> Since *every living thing* follows the pattern of its parentage, are we to suppose that God had some other strange pattern in mind for *His* offspring? Surely we, His children, are not, in the language of science, a different species than He is?
>
> What is in error, then, when we use the term *Godhood* to describe the ultimate destiny of mankind? We may now be young in our progression—juvenile, even infantile, compared with Him. Nevertheless, in the eternities to come, if we are worthy, we may be like unto Him, enter His presence, "see as [we] are seen, and know as [we] are known," and receive a "fulness" (D&C 76:94). . . .
>
> This thought does not fill me with arrogance. It fills me with overwhelming humility. Nor does it sponsor any inclination to worship oneself or any man. . . .
>
> The Father *is* the one true God. *This* thing is certain: no one will ever ascend above Him; no one will ever replace Him. Nor will anything ever change the relationship that we, His literal offspring, have with Him. He is Eloheim, the Father. He is God. Of Him there *is* only one. We revere our

Father and our God; we *worship* Him (*Ensign,* November 1984, pp. 67–68, 69).

Of course, you can't just pull out Elder Packer's talk and hand it to everyone who asks a casual question about our belief in God. But if someone were to show a genuine interest, this is a powerful statement you can paraphrase that beautifully explains why Latter-day Saints are bold enough to believe we have the potential to become gods.

Interestingly, the highly respected Christian author C. S. Lewis also arrived at this conclusion. He has written, "There are no *ordinary* people. . . . It is a serious thing to live in a society of possible gods and goddesses. . . . The dullest and most uninteresting person you can talk to may one day be a creature which, if you saw it now, you would be strongly tempted to worship" (*The Weight of Glory and Other Addresses* [New York: Macmillan, 1980], pp. 18–19).

For me, it is a beautiful thought that we have the potential to one day be exalted. Such an understanding ought to cause us to live more introspectively and to strive always to become better human beings. How inspiring it is to think that though we fall far short of his perfection now, it is our destiny to one day become as he is! We cannot, of course, accomplish all of that on our own. We depend on the Atonement of Jesus Christ and his grace to help us overcome our sinful natures and our many deficiencies. Still, it is a lofty concept and one that suggests how precious and significant every human being is. C. S. Lewis was right: "There are no ordinary people."

Here are some points to remember:

1. The nature of God is not mysterious. We are permitted to know what he is like. Indeed, he has revealed himself to us

through the prophets and the scriptures. He is a tangible being with a body of flesh and bones, and we have been created in his image and likeness.

2. As his spiritually begotten children, we are "heirs of God," with the potential to become like him.

3. As our Father, he will always be greater than us, even if in the eternities we do fulfill our divine potential as his children and become gods.

4. These concepts ought to give us a greater sense of self-worth and make us strive to live better and to expect more from ourselves.

WHY DO MORMONS HAVE LARGE FAMILIES? In the face of expanding world population, many "enlightened" people have concluded it is irresponsible and even immoral to have more than one or two children. It is an issue that has become something of a political football. In Massachusetts, where my husband and I lived for a time, Mormons and Catholics were often lumped together when jokes were made about larger families. These "jokes" sometimes had a bitter edge to them. The implication was, How dare anyone encumber the world's precious resources by bringing even one more human being into the world? Such concerns are often used to justify abortion as a means of birth control, and that, as we have already reviewed, is an issue that divides many Americans along ever-hardening lines.

These are touchy subjects that are tricky to address, yet they are questions that are likely to be asked of us with increasing regularity. We need to be prepared to explain our point of view. I know that I have often been criticized—usually in a joking manner—for choosing to keep having children (and I only have three!) instead of focusing on something a lot more "significant" like a career. Since it is so obvious to me that motherhood *is* the most significant career to focus on, I am shocked by this kind of reasoning.

As for the number of children members of the Church choose to have in their families, this is the counsel given to priesthood leaders for the benefit of the members of the Church:

> "Husbands must be considerate of their wives, who have a great responsibility not only for bearing children but also for caring for them through childhood. . . . Married couples should seek inspiration from the Lord in meeting their marital challenges and rearing their children according to the teachings of the gospel" (*General Handbook [of Instructions],* 11-4).
>
> Interpretation of these general instructions is left to the agency of Church members. One of the basic teachings of the Church, however, is that spirit children of God come to earth to obtain a physical body, to grow, and to be tested. In that process, adults should marry and provide temporal bodies for those spirit children. For Latter-day Saints, it is a blessing, a joy, and also an obligation to bear children and to raise a family (Daniel H. Ludlow, ed., *Encyclopedia of Mormonism,* 4 vols. [New York: Macmillan, 1992], 1:116).

When discussing these matters with someone who expresses an interest, you might begin by pointing out that the Lord instructed Adam and Eve to "be fruitful, and multiply, and replenish the earth" (Genesis 1:28). In keeping that commandment, Mormons have come to cherish children and value families. Indeed, many people are attracted to the Church because of its family orientation.

In a fireside broadcast from the Salt Lake Tabernacle on January 29, 1984, President Gordon B. Hinckley said, "Of course we believe in children. The Lord has told us to multiply and replenish the earth that we might have joy in our posterity, and there is no greater joy than the joy that comes of happy children in good families. But he did not designate the number, nor has the Church. That is a sacred matter left to the couple and the Lord" (Gordon B. Hinckley, *Cornerstones of a Happy Home,* pamphlet [Salt Lake City: Corporation of the President of The Church of Jesus Christ of Latter-day Saints, 1984], p. 6). President Hinckley continued by advising husbands to be considerate of their wives' health and strength in creating a family.

I often include in my answer to those who ask about our tendency toward producing large families my own personal experience and, consequently, my gratitude for large families. I grew up the fifth of seven children and credit my healthy concept of self-worth to being a part of this family in which I developed my strong roots of faith and trust in God. My family members are my best friends in life.

I am also eternally grateful to my in-laws for listening to the Spirit when they were prompted to have just one more child. Blaine and Bonnie Hawkes had nine children in eleven years, and yet, even in this large crowd, they both felt someone was missing. One day Blaine asked Bonnie to go for a walk in the potato fields on their farm near the Tetons in Idaho so they could talk. Bonnie knew exactly what he wanted to talk about. Together they decided that one more spirit was anxious to join the Hawkes family. Were it not for their decision, and the subsequent birth of baby number ten (my husband, Bob), I might still be wandering the earth looking for my soul mate!

As members of the Church, we are taught to study our individual family situations and to take into account the physical and mental health of the mother as well as our capacity to provide the necessities of life. We are not taught that bearing children is the sole function of sexual relations in marriage. We believe that physical intimacy in a marriage enhances the relationship and strengthens the bond between partners and that it is a wholesome, divinely approved part of being married.

As for the idea that the world's natural resources are being depleted, we are grateful for the Lord's own assessment of the matter. He has revealed, "For the earth is full, and there is enough and to spare" (D&C 104:17).

Points to remember:

1. To be a member in good standing, we are not required by the Church to have a family of any specific size. We are expected to prayerfully determine the number of children we can reasonably bear and raise.

2. There are times in marriage when birth control may be appropriate—it is not expressly "forbidden" by Church leadership. Still, we are counseled that having children should not be postponed out of selfishness. This sacred matter should be decided between the couple and the Lord.

3. Many members of the Church do choose to raise large families for several reasons, including obedience to the Lord's commandment to multiply and replenish the earth, a desire to participate in the Plan of Salvation by providing physical bodies for Heavenly Father's spirit children, and the love of children and the joys of family life.

There are, of course, many other questions that might pop up regarding our beliefs and practices—some of them more intricate and sensitive than the ones discussed here and in the next chapter. By thinking in advance of what we really believe, we will perhaps be better prepared to respond when we are asked such questions, and we will enable ourselves to be a guiding light, a beacon, to someone. We ought not to be fearful in this regard. "For God hath not given us the spirit of fear; but of power, and of love, and of a sound mind. Be not thou therefore ashamed of the testimony of our Lord" (1 Timothy 1:7–8).

Recently, my husband and I visited his home ward in St. Anthony, Idaho, where we listened as the Gospel Doctrine teacher related an experience he had in answering multiple questions about the Church at a social gathering. After he had satisfied the curiosity of several guests, one woman approached him and said, "You sound so *sure* of yourself." To which he simply responded, "I *am* sure that the things I have talked about are the absolute truth."

I am convinced that many people admire and are drawn to sincerity and certainty. It has been my experience that whenever we appear even *slightly* hesitant, or apologetic, or embarrassed, we invite cynicism rather than respect. I have often heard my dad suggest that we need to be "sweetly bold" in talking about our beliefs.

CHAPTER 10

MORE ANSWERS TO
FREQUENTLY ASKED QUESTIONS

Every now and then, a well-meaning, curious friend asks me a question that really doesn't require much attention to doctrinal detail because it doesn't have much bearing on our eternal salvation. As such, the question deserves a short, pleasant, and direct answer. Now, may I repeat that the suggestions I would like to offer here are certainly not the only and perhaps not even the best responses possible—just ideas to get you going. And these ideas are based on my own understanding of the Church doctrine and policy, which I formed not only through personal study but also in growing up mostly outside the United States and following my mom and dad around on mission tours and regional conferences and listening to them and many other great leaders of the Church. Also, keep in mind that these answers will obviously work best when put in your own words.

Q: Why do Mormons make such a big deal about avoiding pornography, gambling, swearing, and other such things?

A: The "big deal" is that it's common knowledge these vices lead to bigger problems, bigger sins that only destroy the family and family values. It is part of our creed as members of The Church of Jesus Christ of Latter-day Saints to seek after only things that will serve to make us and the world around us better and better. We seek to build the family and condemn anything that would pull it apart. Pornography, gambling, swearing, and other such things are addictive and destructive. There is nothing quite so pathetic as the secret life led by those who are addicted to pornography; in addition, the number of lives ruined by compulsive gambling are incalculable.

Aside from the adverse social ramifications of becoming addicted to such things, I see pornography, gambling, and profanity as poisons to the human spirit and as barriers that separate us from God. In fact, the closer one gets to God, the more one realizes that there can be no such thing as a "small sin" or a "little transgression." As members of the Church, we choose to avoid that which is ugly and offensive in the world. Instead, as our thirteenth article of faith reminds us, "If there is anything virtuous, lovely, or of good report or praiseworthy, we seek after these things."

Q: Since you belong to the church of Latter-day *Saints,* what saints do you worship?

A: None. In New Testament times, the title *saint* referred to members of Christ's church. Paul wrote his epistles to the saints at Ephesus (or Rome, Corinth, Philippi, etc.). In this dispensation, the Lord revealed that his restored church was to be called The Church of Jesus Christ of Latter-day Saints (see D&C 115:4). It is evident, then, that the word *saint* refers to the followers of Christ and not just those who enjoy special spiritual gifts or who perform miracles. As members of the Church, we consider ourselves Saints in Christ without any pretensions to perfect personal "saintliness." We do not pray to or kneel before any modern or ancient "holy people." We worship only God the Father through the Lord Jesus Christ, and view the Father, the Son, and the Holy Ghost as one Godhead, comprised of three separate and distinct personages.

Q: How can you worship without kneeling in church? I understand you do not even have "kneelers" installed in your pews.

A: We kneel in our homes for family and personal prayer but do not kneel during our sacrament service. Our worship service is called sacrament meeting, and it takes a different form than that of other religions. Please come to church with me next Sunday and see our services for yourself. We worship by singing hymns and by having one of the congregation lead us in prayer (he or she prays vocally in front of the rest of us, and we follow the words silently in our minds). We worship further by partaking each Sunday of the sacrament, consisting of bread and water (not wine), an ordinance by which we recall Christ's suffering in Gethsemane and on the cross and covenant to remember him and keep his commandments. We worship by listening to spontaneous testimonies or prepared talks by members of the congregation, who reflect on Christ and his teachings. Then we close with another hymn and a prayer.

The worship service lasts about an hour, and people of other faiths are welcome to attend. You will not feel awkward or out of place since we do not stand, kneel, or respond verbally to the sermons or proceedings, except by an audible "amen" voiced by the congregation at the conclusion of a talk or the prayers. The worship service is simple, and it provides each person in attendance the opportunity to worship while pondering their commitment to the Savior.

Q: How can you Mormons call yourselves Christians when you don't even display a cross on your buildings?

A: When my husband served as a missionary for my church, he lived in a large metropolitan area that had seen a frightening escalation in violent crime. In answering this question, he would simply ask, "If your brother were shot and killed, would you wear a bullet around your neck to remember him?" We choose spires on our churches to cause us to look upward rather than focus on the symbol of Christ's death. We are Christians because we believe in Christ, viewing him as "the way, the truth, and the life" (John 14:6). It is through Christ that we have the promise of resurrection and the hope (through his grace) of redemption from our sins. "Neither is there salvation in any other: for there is none other name under heaven given among men, whereby we must be saved" (Acts 4:12). We choose to focus on our Savior who *lives,* rather than on a cross where he died. In addition, like the ancient Christians and Jews, we do not believe any man-made object ought to have religious significance. This is in harmony with the Lord's own instructions: "Thou shalt not make unto thee any graven image, or any likeness of any thing that is in heaven above, or that is in the earth beneath, or that is in the water under the earth: Thou shalt not bow down thyself to them, nor serve them" (Exodus 20:4–5). Accordingly, we do not use the cross in our worship, on our buildings, or as jewelry.

Q: How can you say your church is the *only* true church?

A: One of the best answers I have ever heard is from the following address given by Bishop Keith McMullin, second counselor in the Presiding Bishopric, in general conference, April 1996. He said that each of us has been promised, in scripture, that we may know the truth through the sure witness of the Holy Ghost. He told of a friend of his, not a Latter-day Saint, who once asked Bishop McMullin how he could claim that the Church is the only true and living church. Bishop McMullin replied, "I am not claiming it. I am quoting it. Jesus Christ said it." He suggested that if his friend doubted the statement, he should pray and ask Heavenly Father about its truthfulness.

Weeks later, this same friend approached Bishop McMullin after a stake conference:

> The first thought that crossed my mind was, "Oh no, here comes an argument!"
>
> As he approached, he extended his hand and asked, "Do you remember me?"
>
> "I certainly do," I said, "and I want you to know that this is still the only true and living Church."
>
> Before more could be said, his handshake tightened and he replied: "I know! I have prayed about it as you said. The Lord has told me by the power of his Spirit that it is all true. I was baptized last weekend and ordained a priest. Today, I am baptizing my friend here, for he also knows it is true." (*Ensign*, May 1996, pp. 8–9)

Q: It seems there's often weird news that comes out of Utah. Isn't there something a little strange about the way Mormons think and behave?

A: Actually, I wish you could know as I do the many truly wonderful people I have met all over the world who are members of the Church. Surely there are some eccentric and peculiar Mormons, just as there are "peculiar" types in *all* churches. Membership in the Church doesn't guarantee that someone won't have an off-the-wall notion about politics or society or even religion. But there are so many outstanding people I have met, admired, and loved who are members of my church—in South America, in Utah, and everywhere else I have ever lived or traveled. Our congregations are *filled* with beautiful people who are trying hard to live moral lives, to conduct themselves honestly, to raise good children, and to perform charitable acts of many kinds. By and large, Mormons sacrifice to support the Church through the payment of tithes and other offerings. Many volunteer to serve "missions": they leave their homes, families, educational pursuits, and lucrative careers for periods of one to three years. Men and women in the Church accept demanding callings to serve as leaders and teachers in their congregations—serving without any financial remuneration and in a spirit of love and concern. There is no support group in the world to equal a Mormon congregation, a place where the members look to each other's welfare and well-being in a unique and loving way. That is one of the beautiful things about membership in the Church. Please don't judge the Church by the behavior of the few who misrepresent the Church and who don't live up to the standards the Church espouses.

Q: How can you afford to pay tithes to the Church?

A: My oldest daughter, Monica, now six years old, once said to me, "Isn't God nice?" I agreed and asked, "Why do *you* think He is good?" She answered, "He only wants us to give him 10 percent, and he lets us keep the rest!" she hit the nail on the head.

The definition of a tithe (spoken of in the scriptures) *is* one-tenth—that is the amount the Lord intended. All churches depend on donations from their followers. The Lord declared

that his people "shall pay one-tenth of all their interest annually" (D&C 119:4) in support of his church. This is an ancient
law that is mentioned in the Old Testament from Genesis to
Malachi, and so it is not a new notion. The payment of tithing
isn't so much a way of raising money for the operation of the
Church as it is an evidence of faith on the part of the giver.

The "system" is certainly fair and equitable. As a measure
of faith, the widow's mite counts for just as much as the millionaire's large donation. It has been my experience that the
payment of tithing results in blessings from the Lord. Just how
it works is not always clear, but it has been so in my life. When
we pay our tithing, the Lord produces a miracle for us. It defies
mathematics, but the 90 percent that is left after making the
contribution is somehow adequate, whether because the Lord
has blessed us with more income or lower expenses or better
money-management skills. But the formula seems to work best
for those who pay their tithing first. Undoubtedly, that is
because the Lord has promised, "Bring ye all the tithes into the
storehouse, that there may be meat in mine house, and prove
me now herewith, saith the Lord of hosts, if I will not open you
the windows of heaven, and pour you out a blessing, that there
shall not be room enough to receive it" (Malachi 3:10). Many
members of the Church feel that they can't afford *not* to pay
their tithing.

Q: Why do you Mormons wear such weird underwear?

A: The undergarment many Mormons wear is to remind
us of the commitments we have made to keep the Lord's commandments and to be true to our religion. These garments are
very sacred to me, and so I don't speak of them lightly. They

are outward symbols and reminders of inward covenants we make to remember and dedicate our lives to Christ.

My dad was once invited by his boss to play golf at an exclusive country club in South America. They had come directly to the course from the office and planned to change into their golf clothes at the club. Dad had assumed there would be some privacy, but to his surprise, the dressing area was totally open.

Upon observing Dad's one-piece undergarment, his host inquired simply, "What is that you are wearing?" Dad answered, "I am an ordained minister in my church and this is part of our ministerial robes, which we wear on the inside, not the outside . . . more democratic. In fact, all committed adult members of the Church wear these as well to remind ourselves of our commitments to the Lord." The explanation was accepted without question.

Regardless of the question, even regardless of the seemingly thoughtless intent of the curious, *any* honest inquiry about the Church can provide an opportunity to share something of our beliefs. We don't have to give more information than is needed on sensitive subjects, but if we are imaginative, we can almost always use such an inquiry to generate a gospel discussion. We might say, "You obviously know a little bit about the Mormons; would you like to know more?" Without being overbearing, we can turn such a setting into an opportunity to introduce someone to our beliefs or present a copy of the Book of Mormon.

As our prophet, President Gordon B. Hinckley, closed the final session of the April 1996 general conference, he told us of his decision to allow the CBS crew of *60 Minutes* to spend extensive time with him and many other members of the Church for a report that would air that evening. He admitted that he had no idea whether this report would be favorable or filled with sound bytes from critics of the Church.

However, President Hinckley concluded that it was better to "lean into the stiff wind of opportunity than to simply hunker down and do nothing." He then said that if the program "turns out to be favorable [toward the Church] I will be grateful. Otherwise, I pledge I'll never get my foot in that kind of trap again" (*Ensign,* May 1996, p. 83). That willingness to be bold in the face of possible criticism, even perhaps disdain, is an example from our prophet that we should all seek to follow. Sure, it is risky to cast your pearls out, never really certain whether they will be trampled in the mud or picked up and cherished. Most often, it seems, it is the former. Our 50,000-plus missionaries who serve all over the world know all too well the discouragement, sometimes embarrassment, that comes from rejection. But again, it is better to "lean into the stiff wind of opportunity than to simply hunker down and do nothing." Why? Well, what purpose is served by hunkering down? It's the same thing as hiding our light under a bushel. And if we are discouraged or embarrassed by someone's less-than-receptive attitude to our answers, what is the worst that can happen? They can joke, make fun, tease. They can walk away. What is the best that can happen? They can nod their heads and perhaps say, "I'd like to know more." "Lean into the stiff wind," for there is far more to gain from it. Not surprisingly, our prophet leads the way.

As many watched the program on a nationwide network that night, it was clear that veteran reporter Mike Wallace liked the things he had seen and heard. Our prophet's decision to host this network TV crew had, in the end, produced an unexpectedly flattering look at "the Mormons." One of the reasons I believe Mr. Wallace maintained a positive demeanor throughout the feature was due to the nondefiant and sometimes humorous manner in which his questions were answered.

There is nothing better than a sense of humor to diffuse a potentially awkward situation. When, in the same program, Mr. Wallace interviewed San Francisco 49er star quarterback Steve Young about the "sacred undergarments," Steve recalled the good-natured ribbing he had taken from his teammates because of them. He told Mr. Wallace that when they ask where he gets the "undergarments," he simply responds, "They're too expensive for you!" Mike Wallace really got a laugh out of Steve's response, especially in light of the question he had just asked the prominent Mormon about the payment of tithing—a hefty sum for a professional athlete of Steve's caliber!

Steve is a seasoned pro, not only in football but in dealing with the media. He has had years of practice in fielding questions about his religion, and he has learned the best ways to respond. We can learn much from the congenial way he handles difficult questions. He has a knack for not taking himself too seriously, and he doesn't become defensive. Steve also is direct and sincere and makes effective use of his sense of humor. He is a wonderful representative for us Church members.

Throughout the *60 Minutes* program, President Gordon B. Hinckley was able to virtually dissolve any criticism that surfaced because his responses were forthright and laced with his

good-natured and sincere manner. His answers were remark-
ably brief—a pattern we might all follow. He didn't permit
himself to be drawn into a discussion of controversial topics.
Instead, he emphasized the positive things the Church teaches
and the blessing the gospel represents in people's lives.
Throughout their interchange, President Hinckley obviously
had Mr. Wallace's full attention. The veteran reporter
responded warmly to the prophet's wit and charm, but he was
also visibly moved by President Hinckley's expressions of faith
and his teachings. Our prophet and president met every challenge and was a perfect role model of how members of the
Church can serve as powerful beacon lights in a world filled
with uncertainty and doubt. He demonstrated in textbook
fashion how to face the world head-on: always with dignity,
with assurance, and especially with a congenial demeanor.

CHAPTER 11

SHOULD MORMONS CHOOSE TO LIVE IN "BABYLON"?

My parents lived in Latin America for over thirty years, raised seven children successfully, and enjoyed both a banking career and a Church ministry there, far from the center stakes of Zion. My oldest sister and her family live in the Philippine Islands, my two brothers have worked most of their careers in the Midwest of the United States, and two other sisters and their families live and work in California. On the other hand, after living back East for a while, my husband and I made the decision to move and to raise our family in Utah. Because I grew up so far away from extended members of my family, and with our family moving every few years, I was eager to see what it was like to stay in one place for a while and spend time around family. Since my husband and I agree there are distinct advantages to both child-hood scenarios, it was not a "wrong versus right" decision. It just felt appropriate for us at the time. Each individual and fam-ily has to make their own decisions on these matters. Every sit-uation is different. Just don't make a decision based on fear of the unknown.

Mom and Dad have also lived at various times in New York City and in Las Vegas. Dad was born in Las Vegas, and he began his banking career there as a courier, carrying bags of silver dollars up and down famous Fremont Street (the "Strip") to the various casinos. He also worked for a time in "The Big Apple"—New York City—on Wall Street, gaining his early training in international banking there. Mom was born and raised in El Paso, Texas, where she had many opportunities to share the gospel with non-LDS friends.

My parents have frequently been asked such questions as "When you choose to live in foreign countries or big cities with high crime rates, or any area where the Church is less established than in Utah, don't you run a huge risk of losing your family to the world?" and "Isn't it harder to raise children with LDS standards away from the center stakes of Zion?" and "Aren't temptations of the world greater when local Church units are small and struggling, are trying to get along with poorly trained leaders, and are meeting in substandard facilities?"

Those who ask such questions probably assume that where Church units are extremely well organized, parents will be better able to save their children from "Babylon"—the worldly atmosphere of most locales with predominantly non-LDS populations—and from Satan's grasp. They may also believe that where the Church is more prominently established, testimonies of the members are stronger and the presence of the Spirit is more profoundly felt.

It has been our family's experience that it is in many ways better, easier, and safer to raise children in the midst of "Babylon" than it is in the heart of Zion. I can almost hear gasps of astonishment from many who read that statement. It sounds almost like heresy or abject apostasy. Please let me explain.

No matter what the environment, some children seem to get into trouble. Others, however, never seem to be drawn into evil paths, regardless of how much wickedness surrounds them. There have been some prodigals and lost sheep since the beginning of time. But the greatest protection for children is found in parental concern and the level of spirituality inside their home.

In the case of our family, we almost always lived in places where there were no organized Scout troops, no elaborate chapels, no experienced, longtime members to serve as teachers or leaders, and so on. Our spiritual learning was much more dependent on our parents, and our testimonies were strengthened constantly by the daily opportunities we had to either share or defend our faith. In particular, our perspectives were shaped by the diversity we encountered in the members of our various wards—many of them relatively recent converts with burning enthusiasm for their newfound faith. That alone was a wonderful attitude that rubbed off on us!

The home where family prayer is the pattern—and where fasting, the payment of tithes, scripture reading, and faith and devotion are taught—usually produces children who can resist temptations. When parents provide an environment that is free of profanity or physical, verbal, or sexual abuse, and when the home is a place where Sabbath observance is taught and practiced, where the Word of Wisdom is lived, and where the parents live to be worthy of their temple recommends, children can grow up fortified against the world. Children reared in such homes are usually able to resist temptations, even if all kinds of sin and vice surround them in their schools and neighborhoods.

Growing up in such a home and living in a place where Mormons were in the minority, my siblings and I all sensed that we were in the spotlight. We sensed the need to live up to our standards, to be examples to our friends. In fact, in many instances, our friends of other faiths knew what was expected of us, and they simply wouldn't allow us to compromise, even if we had been so inclined.

Another factor that tended to help us live our religion was the feeling that we did not want to disappoint our parents or the Lord. We felt loved and trusted, and we wanted to measure up. Even though there were periods of typical teenage defiance, we wanted to be good members of the Church because our parents had taught us the gospel, provided us with a good example, and helped us to learn to love the Lord—in our home.

Having observed LDS families living overseas for many years, my parents have told me that they see no more risk living out in the world where the Church is not well established than it would be to raise their children right in the middle of the strongest stakes of the Church. As a child and a teenager, I found it much easier to live the gospel in areas where the Church wasn't predominant. In those areas, everything was black and white—my standards were clear, "their" standards were clear—there was no gray.

Dad knew of one LDS engineer who turned down a lucrative job offer because it would have meant taking his family to the interior of a remote country. The man feared raising his children in a place where there would be no Aaronic Priesthood quorums, no Primary, no Scouting, no Sunday School, etc. He and his wife were concerned at the idea of being the sole teachers of righteousness to their children. But perhaps he passed up an ideal opportunity to become an "Abraham" in the desert and a true patriarch to his family, as well as the first or only LDS person many in that country might have ever met. He could have obtained permission to hold weekly sacrament meetings in their home, and, using Church-produced manuals, he could have become the principal teacher of the gospel to his children. He could have turned his home into the first branch of the Church in that location and done all kinds of good missionary work. And his children may well have been strengthened by the experience.

When we face similar choices, we need to be prayerful and wise, listening for spiritual guidance. Friends and relatives may offer plentiful advice—"Go, it'll be a great adventure!" or "Don't risk your family's salvation by leaving a predominantly LDS area for one where Latter-day Saints are scarce!" If we ask the Lord sincerely, weighing matters in our minds, he will help us make wise decisions by which the whole family will be blessed.

My mom and dad say they had more problems holding the line after we returned to Utah than they ever had while living overseas. In the places where we lived away from the center of the Church, my brothers and sisters and I were often the only LDS kids in the school, as I have mentioned. We encountered Jews, Muslims, Protestants, Catholics, and Buddhists where we lived. We were willing to be different—in part because it was normal to be different. Each group had its peculiarities—different holidays, dietary limitations, and unique religious practices. Therefore, it was okay to be LDS and different. We found a great deal of tolerance, and no one ridiculed us after we explained what we believed and the things we practiced; neither did we ridicule them for their practices.

When I was seven years old, we moved to Utah for a time, and there we found circumstances more challenging. There was a great deal of diversity in the degree of strictness of LDS parents in our ward and stake. Some parents seemed very liberal. The fad at the time was to wear short skirts. Mom and Dad thought the style was immodest, but it was difficult for them to enforce what they thought was an appropriate dress length when other LDS kids were allowed to wear shorter skirts. My older sisters raised what they thought was a valid argument by saying, "Dad and Mom, have you noticed the length of the skirts worn by [this or that Church leader's] daughter?" The same thing happened over the length of my brothers' hair. Mom and Dad thought the boys ought to get their hair cut shorter, but the boys countered by saying, "Have you checked out the hair length of the sons of some of our stake leaders?" Our parents lost the argument in some instances. What they found was that while living overseas, a family standard could be established without encountering much resistance from their children, but living in Utah, where there was such a diversity of opinion among members of the Church, it was difficult to be the most conservative family in the ward or stake.

I recall an incident that took place during my senior year in high school. We had recently returned to the United States after four years in Buenos Aires, Argentina. I asked my dad if I could participate in some activity on a Sunday with a friend—I don't remember what or with whom. Dad felt it was an inappropriate thing to do on the Sabbath and therefore said no. I countered by saying, "But *she's* going, and her dad's a bishop."

Dad calmly replied, "There's a world standard, there's a Church standard, and there's a Wells family standard—and that's the one we go by."

Of course, one of the greatest benefits of growing up away from large concentrations of Mormons was the opportunity to do missionary work. We often had to walk a fine line, particularly in school. We could not preach the gospel too directly because we could easily have isolated ourselves or alienated potential friends. On the other hand, we were at liberty to stand up for our beliefs and standards, and that often attracted favorable attention. By praying for opportunities and being alert to the right moment, we were able to introduce the gospel to many.

Living in the more remote areas from Church headquarters—the "mission field," as we used to call it—also put us in close touch with the full-time missionaries, who were wonderful role models and examples for us kids. We were often given the chance to go out with the sister missionaries on "splits" to visit their investigators and to participate and learn as they taught the gospel to their contacts. These kinds of opportunities are plentiful out in the world but are only infrequently available in places where there is a heavy concentration of members.

In the Old Testament, the young prophet Daniel was taken captive into Babylon by King Nebuchadnezzar. It goes without saying that it was not his choice to live in Babylon or to be a servant in the king's court. Doubtless, Daniel would have preferred to continue living in Jerusalem with his loved ones and in familiar, comfortable surroundings.

Instead, he found himself living in a foreign country and having to choose between two conflicting lifestyles. He could have turned his back on the teachings of his youth and adopted the ways of the Babylonians. He might have wallowed in self-pity or blamed God for allowing him to be in such a place. He did none of that. So how did a young Jewish man, carried captive into Babylon, eventually become "chief of the wise men, chancellor of the equivalent of a national university, ruler of all the Hebrew captives, and, as a governor of the province of Babylon, one of the chief rulers in both the Babylonian and Persian empires"? (*Old Testament Student Manual* [Salt Lake City: The Church of Jesus Christ of Latter-day Saints, 1981], p. 28).

Though Daniel lived in the heart of Babylon, Babylon had no success whatsoever in destroying Daniel's spirit. He succeeded because he remained righteous and sensitive to the promptings of the Spirit. The gospel was his fortress that kept out anyone and anything that could have destroyed his life's mission. President Spencer W. Kimball said this about Daniel:

> The gospel was Daniel's life. The Word of Wisdom was vital to him. In the king's court, he could be little criticized, but even for a ruler he would not drink the king's wine nor gorge himself with meat and rich foods. His moderation and his purity of faith brought him health and wisdom and knowledge and skill and understanding, and his faith linked him closely to his Father in heaven, and revelations came to him as often as required. His revealing of the dreams of the king and the interpretations thereof brought him honor and acclaim and gifts and high position such as many men would sell their souls to get. (Conference Report, Mexico and Central America Area Conference, 1972, p. 31)

Living as members of a "minority" group provides a tremendous opportunity to serve and teach if we seek the direction of the Spirit as did Ammon, another scriptural hero. He was an example of one who went into a strange land and, through service and the exercise of the pure love of Christ, exerted a righteous influence. He gained the confidence of the Lamanites and touched their hearts. Ammon held to his beliefs, and the strangers among whom he lived ended up adopting his standards and his way of life. He didn't leave his beliefs at the border, and he didn't alter what he stood for because he was afraid of what people might think of him. Ammon left his "comfort zone" and put himself in a place where he could make a vital difference.

Perhaps you don't *choose* to live "in the world," outside your comfort zone. Perhaps the only job opportunity available is the one that takes you far away from everything familiar. But no matter the circumstance—whether you're in army barracks or in a university dormitory, in a smoke-filled business meeting in Europe or a greasy truck-stop diner on an unfamiliar highway—the gospel is your shield. And it is a friendly shield. It protects us from unwanted barbs and keeps us safe from a constantly changing and fickle world. When others seek after that safety and peace we have found, the shield widens to include and protect them as well.

There are many benefits to living away from the centers of the Church—benefits that offset the advantages of living in predominantly LDS communities—when you measure the lifetime results.

The question really becomes how to effectively live the gospel in our own homes, no matter where those homes are located in the world. President David O. McKay said, "No other success can compensate for failure in the home."

President Harold B. Lee said, "The most important of the Lord's work you will ever do will be within the walls of your own homes." And President Spencer W. Kimball taught us, "Our success, individually and as a church, will largely be determined by how faithfully we focus on living the gospel in the home" (see Conference Report, April 1964, p. 5; "Be Loyal to the Royal Within You," *Speeches of the Year, 1973* [Provo: BYU Press, 1974], 11 September 1973; *Ensign,* May 1978, p. 100).

Homes are more important than chapels. The Prophet Joseph Smith never built a chapel in New York, or Missouri, or Illinois. He placed his entire emphasis on temples and a home-focused religion in which the members were taught to worship Jesus Christ and our Heavenly Father. The home and the temple. What a powerful combination! Because our children can't be taught in the temple in their early years, the home alone has to be strong enough to save our children. In the home we can instill in them the desire to receive temple endowments, go on a mission, and be married in the temple.

Some parents understandably feel inadequate and not at all confident in their ability to make their home a celestial abode, so pure and filled with righteousness that Satan cannot destroy or lead their children astray. They may feel that they are not skilled enough as teachers to accomplish that goal. We all feel that way. In the face of gangs, violence, and the ugliness often portrayed on television and in the movies, there is much to overcome. Sure, some neighborhoods have more trouble than others, and it may be necessary in some instances to move when improvements can't be made. But taking an active interest in local politics, school PTAs, and neighborhood action groups can do much to improve our circumstances wherever we are.

I agree with my parents and the thousands of LDS people I have met in my travels who have successfully met the challenge of raising good families in the midst of a "Babylon." It is possible, it is exciting, it is an adventure, and it can be enormously satisfying on a spiritual level. You *can* live in the world and remain worthy of a temple recommend. And in such dark places your beacon light can shine even brighter.

CHAPTER 12

THE POWER OF A REPUTATION

I have worked for ESPN since 1988—full-time for the first two years, then part-time until our children were born, at which time I became more of a freelance contributor. From 1990 to 1994, I was one of their college football "regular" reporters. My assignments took me to such traditional campuses as Notre Dame, Penn State, Ohio State, and Tennessee, to name just a few. Once, I was sent to the University of Alabama to produce a feature on the number-one team in the nation at that time. This was the university where the legendary coach Paul "Bear" Bryant made his mark. I had never visited the campus before, and I looked forward to meeting and interviewing the head football coach, Gene Stallings.

Coach Stallings invited us to interview him in his office—a beautiful, well-decorated room easily four or five times the size of BYU coach LaVell Edwards's office. Such interviews were normally conducted in a conference room, so we naturally felt privileged to have been invited in there. The coach was at a meeting while we set up our cameras and equipment. When he arrived, I found him easy to converse with and took an instant liking to him.

The interview lasted about twenty minutes, and when we were finished, I expected him to rush off. Instead, he continued to chat as the crew was packing up the lights, tripod, and electrical cords. He asked where we were from, and when I said that I was from Utah, he was curious about where I had gone to school.

"I'm a BYU grad," I said proudly.

"Is that so? Well, I have tremendous respect for LaVell Edwards. He is an excellent coach and a wonderful human being."

I expected that kind of response. Every football coach I had ever talked to, upon learning I was a BYU alum, had some kind of compliment for Coach Edwards. In fact, Penn State Coach Joe Paterno had said almost exactly the same thing to me as Coach Stallings did. As always, I was grateful for LaVell's impeccable reputation and for making all us Mormons look good.

Then Coach Stallings asked me if I too was a Mormon. Because most conversations that take place in a football coach's office are not about religion, all six people in the room stopped what they were doing to listen to my answer.

"Yes, sir, I am."

"Well," he said, "then I have a story for you."

He proceeded to recount an experience his brother had shared with him. His brother had attended a business convention. One of the topics that came up for discussion was how to prevent theft by employees. Some of the participants had described their "horror" stories about these kinds of losses, each one a little worse than the one before. It was a big problem and one that seemed to affect them all.

Finally, the group leader asked if anyone had any suggestions about how to remedy the problem. Several suggestions were made. Then Coach Stallings's brother said that in his company they had discovered a foolproof way to prevent employee theft. He told the group that since they had implemented this plan, there had not been one item missing from his inventory. Of course, the managers all leaned forward, eager to hear his solution.

"I hire only Mormons," he said.

When Coach Stallings finished telling his story, he chuckled along with the rest of us, and then added, "That says a lot for you people."

Naturally, I felt a sense of pride and gratitude toward those who were living the standards of the Church, but then I had another thought: It was likely that his favorable opinion of us Mormons would hold up only until he met a Mormon who *failed* to live up to that reputation. His positive feelings about us could easily be turned negative if he met and was disappointed by just one member of the Church.

Every one of us has a reputation, for good or bad. Whatever our role—employee, student, parent, business executive—our associates have evaluated us and we have been branded. The question is, what *kind* of reputation have we acquired?

When my family moved from Argentina back to Salt Lake City, I was midway through my junior year in high school. I remember a powerful lesson I learned on the first day of school. It was a lesson about reputations.

I started school that morning not knowing a soul except my sister Elayne. Together we wandered the halls, feeling very much the outsiders, searching for classrooms and our lockers. We were concerned about making a new start in the middle of our high school experience and nervous about making new friends. We were anxious to be accepted and to be liked. But Skyline High School in Salt Lake City was huge compared to the high school we had recently left in Buenos Aires. There, I had known all of the 150 or so students, but now—well, there were about 600 kids in my grade alone! It was pretty intimidating, and we were sure that no one would even notice us.

However, in my first class, I was instantly made comfortable when two girls seated nearby went out of their way to welcome me. They recognized I was new and asked me where I had moved from. So many people walked the halls that I was surprised that they could tell I was new. How could they tell the difference? At the time I thought they were just especially observant. Later I learned that these were popular girls who knew just about everyone in the school. When I walked in, they naturally and correctly assumed that since they didn't know who I was, I must be a newcomer.

They asked if I would like to sit with them during lunch, and I readily accepted the invitation. Elayne had been assigned a different lunch break, so I was relieved not to have to eat alone.

When I walked into the cafeteria, my new friends were already sitting at a table near the door. They waved me over, and it felt good to have someone in the vast sea of new classmates know my name.

While we were waiting in line for the school lunch, my new friends introduced me to nearly everybody who walked by. I was terribly impressed by how many people they knew!

When we sat down to eat, the introductions kept right on coming, only this time the introductions were tinged with commentary. My new friends not only knew everyone by name, they knew them also by *reputation*.

"That's _____. She's stuck up"; "And that's _____. We call him 'Mr. Octopus.' You don't want to go out with him."

"There's _____. He's really friendly and a genuinely nice guy" and "That girl's name is _____. You can't get a straight answer out of her. She lies about everything" and "Oh, _____ is nice to your face, but you wouldn't believe the kinds of things she'll say behind your back." And so on.

It made me think. I wondered what they would say about *me*—but I wasn't thinking about their judgmental comments, really. They weren't saying anything in a mean or gossipy way, just being frank. No, I was much more concerned about *my* reputation. And I thought about the advantage I had: because it was my first day at school, my slate was clean. No one knew me, and therefore I didn't have a reputation yet. I was excited to know that I was largely in charge of what my reputation would be. *Here's a chance to write a description of the kind of person I would like to be!* I thought.

One of the things I quickly noticed was how each person's reputation is also colored by the people they go around with. Their behavior reflects on us, just as our behavior reflects on them. Our parents, siblings, spouses, best friends, teachers, and co-workers—all are in some way affected by the way we choose to live our lives. What we say and do truly rubs off on each other—for good or bad.

The dating scene is a good place to observe this. When I was in high school, I met and began dating a young man from a neighboring school. He immediately impressed me with his honesty, integrity, strength of character, testimony—not to mention his good looks. I had no doubt that when I met his family, they would be the same. It turned out to be so, and I was equally impressed with his parents and twelve brothers and sisters. I continue to admire the entire family as a result of the positive behavior of their older brother.

On the other hand, later when I was in college, I briefly dated a young man whom I soon discovered to be rude, unkind, and irresponsible. Not long after my last date with this character, I met his brother. He seemed nice enough, but it was hard for me to imagine him being much different from his brother. I found myself avoiding him simply because he was related to someone I tried to avoid. For all I know, he might have been the complete opposite and quite a catch. But, unfair as it was, I had already labeled him based on his brother's behavior, and I did not want to take the chance of dating another like him.

Whether we like it or not, we do represent more than just ourselves. When we leave our home, we represent our family. When we attend high school, we represent our school, our teachers, and our classmates. When we enroll in college, we represent our institution. When we travel, we represent our state and our nation. Observing us, the world will judge those we represent. How we conduct ourselves will reflect on where we come from. This is particularly true with regard to our membership in The Church of Jesus Christ of Latter-day Saints. One individual has the capacity to leave an indelible impression—for good or bad—on literally everyone with whom he or she comes in contact.

I have noticed that when some Church members travel on business or vacation, they change their behavior. They leave their standards at home along with their scriptures. It is almost as if they say to themselves: "No one knows me here! Why not have a drink, why not get rid of the garments, why not play on Sunday, why not watch pornography, and why not gamble?"

I have often heard my dad tell the story of a returned missionary who was attending college in California. He joined a popular social fraternity and soon became an officer in it, a position that gave him the chance to help plan the activities. In spite of his background, he turned his back on the duties of his Church membership, and he began drinking socially with his buddies.

It was the beginning of a new school year, and the initiation rites for the fraternity were now underway. An activity designed to haze the freshmen turned tragic, and one of the pledges died as a result of the irresponsible and senseless requirement.

The university took immediate action by suspending the leaders of the fraternity for their part in planning such a dangerous prank. However, only one leader, the returned missionary, was expelled with the stipulation that he could never return as a student to that campus.

The young man and his father were angry as they stood before the president of the university. They argued that the school was guilty of religious discrimination because he, a member of the LDS church, was the only one expelled, even though others were equally to blame for the tragedy.

The university president remained unmoved. "We know of your standards and the training you have received," he began. "You know better than to be involved in anything this irresponsible and dangerous. We expect more of you. We want no student on our campus who would turn his back on such knowledge."

My dad also tells of a large corporation that routinely hired returned LDS missionaries who had language skills the company could use in its international operations. Each newly hired employee would be given a few months' experience and training in company policies and procedures, then be sent overseas. The jobs were prestigious and paid very well.

Once, halfway through the training program, the company fired one of the returned missionaries. This was a source of embarrassment to the other LDS employees because his failure affected their reputations too. The head of the firm later explained, "We have always had great success hiring Mormons. But we noticed that your colleague was a clock-watcher. He arrived exactly at eight o'clock in the morning and left promptly at five o'clock in the afternoon. You Mormons have always arrived early and left late. We decided we did not want a substandard Mormon. There might have been other weaknesses that would show up later."

During the year I served as Miss America, I traveled the country and also abroad. In many places I had the opportunity to speak to LDS groups. After speaking, I would usually invite the audience to ask questions. I loved responding to their inquiries, and the one that popped up most often was, "How much of a burden is it to represent the Church?"

Early in the year, I used to tell the audience that, yes, I did feel pressured by having to answer so many Church-related questions. I felt a heavy responsibility to answer everything correctly. I was concerned about accurately stating our beliefs or the Church's position on various topics. I didn't want to say anything careless that might end up as a headline, thus embarrassing the Church.

A few months into the Miss America year, I had an experience that made me realize more fully how visible *all* Mormons are. During a flight to the West Coast, I was reading an article in the newspaper about a man who had been convicted of large-scale fraud. It was an average see-what's-wrong-with-the-world article, except that in recounting the facts of the case, the reporter made a point of identifying the criminal as a Mormon. I wondered how come these kinds of articles rarely report the religious affiliation of anybody except Mormons.

I suppose, in a way, it is a compliment to have the Church named—as though it is unusual for a Mormon to be involved in such a crime. But at that moment, I did not view it as any sort of a compliment. I was embarrassed and ashamed. I did not know the man. I had never heard of him, and yet his choices had an effect on *me*. I hoped no one else would see the article and lump all of us Mormons into one category. But sure enough, my traveling companion was reading the same newspaper, and she spotted the story.

Leaning over to show me the article, she whispered, "Hey, did you read about the Mormon convicted of fraud?" You see, just by being a Mormon, we are viewed by the world as belonging to the same family, and she thought I would be interested to know what my "brother" had been up to.

"Yeah, I saw it. Don't remind me," I joked back at her, trying not to make a big deal out of it. I was not proud of my "relative" right then, and I knew what I would say the next time I was asked if it is a burden to represent the Church.

At the next fireside, I did alter my response. I told them

everything I had been saying about having to be careful to avoid being misinterpreted. Then I told the audience what I had learned from reading about the Mormon who had been convicted of fraudulent behavior. I told them that every single one of us is a representative of the Church and of the gospel of Jesus Christ. Most of us don't wear name tags, and we may not hold news conferences, but each of us has a responsibility to be an exemplary member of the Church. If we are not, it can have an enormous negative impact on all those who are trying to live the standard. I concluded my remarks by saying the burden of representing the Church well does not rest on any *one* of us, but on *all* of us. I pledged my best efforts not to do or say anything that would reflect negatively on the Church and challenged them to do the same.

Whenever I would visit a new town and someone would say, "Hey, I know a Mormon!" I would hold my breath, waiting to hear what would be said next. More often than not, it was positive, and I would feel proud to be a Mormon as well. But when the report was not favorable, there wasn't much I could do but express my regrets and feel uncomfortable.

Depending on where we live and what our circumstances are, some of us may encounter negative feelings toward the Church more often than others. Sometimes how we are perceived is due to an anti-Mormon feeling that prevails in some places. Or perhaps we send unintentional messages to our friends because of the way we act. But whatever the cause, impressions are real to those who hold them. And while we can't do much to change stories that are fabricated or truths that are stretched, we certainly can take an inward look and evaluate what we might be doing to contribute to negative feelings toward the Church.

One of the problems we sometimes have as members of the Church is a tendency to come across as "holier than thou." While we are never justified in feeling superior to those of other faiths, we tend to view ourselves as having more direct access to Heavenly Father because we are members of the restored Church. Sometimes we make a poor impression because when we choose to proclaim our standards, we thoughtlessly refer to them as higher standards. There is no question that there is much that is evil in the world, but I have found there is also much goodness, and we Mormons aren't the only ones trying to live righteous lives. The world is filled with honorable, decent people who are understandably offended when we suggest we are somehow spiritually superior to them. When Jesus walked the earth, he condemned that kind of pride in those he met.

Members of the Church are sometimes guilty of another kind of self-righteous, offensive attitude. I'm talking about intolerance. Some of us have a tendency to judge the behavior of others too harshly. We see others smoking or using alcohol or breaking some other commandment, and we jump to the conclusion that they are bad people. Some of us are so narrow-minded that we dismiss anyone who is not a Mormon, reasoning that if they belong to some other church they must somehow be spiritually deficient. I have met many of other faiths who are every bit as in tune with the Spirit as some active members of the LDS faith—sometimes even more so.

Last year during the Christmas season, I encouraged a non-LDS friend of mine to take her family to see the lights on

Temple Square. I suggested that it would be a fun family activity, but she immediately wrinkled her nose and shook her head to this idea. I was surprised to learn that she had never been to Temple Square though she had lived in Salt Lake City all her life. Her reason? She had been treated rudely by most members of the Church with whom she had come in contact and was therefore not only completely uninterested in anything to do with the Mormons but would deliberately avoid any event or location sponsored by the Church. I really couldn't believe that so many members had been the cause of such disdain, but she insisted that Mormon neighbors would not allow their children to interact with hers, that Mormon clients were cool and patronizing, and that she had been shunned all through high school by Mormon students.

My guess is that we don't intend to come across as a myopic people, but perhaps our behavior could be interpreted as such when we distance ourselves and focus only on "the members," or when we judge others according to our belief system. I was told of a member who, in the midst of a gossip session concerning a neighbor of another faith, exclaimed in dismay, "And did you know that when their church is over, they serve doughnuts and *coffee?*" It was as if to say, "Now, how can they possibly claim to be good people!"

One of my sisters, who lives outside of Utah, made what I thought was an extremely valid and insightful comment. She said we Mormons tend to be so focused on "carrying the banner high, proclaiming the message of the gospel, etc." that we sometimes forget to simply reach out and love our neighbors *just because that is the Christian thing to do* and not because we have to convert everyone in our path.

We need to evaluate ourselves. Are we doing or saying anything, even if our intentions are pure, that might alienate those around us? Do we imply that we are better than others because we have "higher standards"? How can we be more *Christian* as well as "Mormon"? Again, we are continually creating an impression on those who watch us, and that impression usually becomes the standard by which outsiders judge the Church.

There is one colleague of mine, in particular, for whom I have the highest regard. We became acquainted years ago, and I recall he had a growing interest in the Church. He would occasionally ask me a question about our beliefs, but his busy lifestyle prevented him from any serious study of the gospel. I changed jobs but kept track of him and was thrilled to learn that he eventually married a member of the Church. I assumed his interest in the gospel was growing by leaps and bounds. Through the grapevine, I even heard that he was occasionally attending meetings of the Church.

Not too long ago, however, I ran into his mother-in-law. I was interested in how my friend was doing, but when I asked about him, her smile quickly faded. She told me that he had lost all interest and was no longer taking the discussions. Of course, I was astonished. What could have happened to change his mind so drastically?

She explained that, yes, he had been attending church and had been asking a lot of good questions, but that it was the influence of some of his colleagues at work that had changed his mind. These people were not anti-Mormons who gave him persuasive literature or otherwise poisoned his mind; rather, these were supposedly active members of the Church who, by the *negative* power of their examples and hypocritical behavior, had turned him away from the gospel.

But on a more positive note, for every story like my friend's, I know twenty other accounts of people who initially became interested in the Church and were subsequently baptized because of the positive influence of Mormons they encountered and admired. When my husband and I were living in Massachusetts, we met a young woman in our ward who had recently joined the Church. She told us she had sought out the missionaries to learn more about the Church because of her deep admiration for Dale Murphy and the way he conducted his public and private life. She was a huge baseball fan and had followed Dale's career for years. His example had influenced her just as he no doubt influenced many others for good during his long and successful professional baseball career.

Let me relate another example. I first met Vern and Luana Brazell and their family during my junior year in high school. The Brazells lived in our ward in Salt Lake City, and through a shared love of missionary work, our two families became fast friends. In the fifteen years or so that I have known them, I have been proud of their exemplary conduct both among members of the Church and in their other associations. Sharing the gospel has literally been their life's mission. Vern and Luana have opened their home to countless people of all backgrounds, inviting people they had just met to come to their home for dinner or even to live with them if the people needed a place to stay. It has also been their family's practice to let everyone they meet know how important the gospel is in their lives. Yet they do not preach; they simply live the gospel and let their example do the rest.

A few years ago, Vern was asked to host a man from Taiwan who was flying into Salt Lake City to do some computer work for the Church. He was a top engineer, but he spoke very little English and was not a member of the Church. He was to be in town for ten days, and the original plan was to have him check into a hotel for his stay. But his plane arrived quite late, and it seemed easier for the Brazells to take him to their home instead of to the hotel that first night.

The Brazells' youngest son, Troy, who had recently returned from his mission to Japan, found it enjoyable to try and converse with their guest. Hoping to learn more of this man's language, Troy somehow convinced the man to stay just one more night. He ended up staying with the Brazells for the whole ten days.

The family never cornered their new friend in an attempt to explain their LDS views and beliefs. They didn't exert an ounce of pressure on him. Instead, they simply included the man in their family prayers, scripture study, and family home evening activities. Vern and Luana also invited him to go with them to a Relief Society retreat where he was able to observe the workings of the Church's women's organization. He was impressed by what he saw and felt.

After completing his business in Salt Lake, the man returned directly to Taiwan, and, unbeknownst to the Brazells, quickly sought out the missionaries. One of Vern's business associates who was based in Taiwan happened to be in Salt Lake City some months later and reported he had seen the man. In fact, Vern's colleague had attended a dinner where the Brazells' friend was present, and while all around him were indulging in alcoholic drinks, their former houseguest had been overheard to say, "No. I do not drink, because I am a Mormon!"

Naturally, Vern was thrilled at the news and said he was unaware the man from Taiwan had joined the Church. His colleague informed Vern that his friend had been baptized shortly after returning home from his stay in the Brazells' home. Later on, the missionaries who had taught the man contacted Vern and Luana and explained that their friend had expressed his desire to have for his family what he had observed in the Brazells' home.

When I spoke with Luana recently, she told me, "We try to provide our friends with an opportunity to experience the gospel. They come when they are ready, and we let *them* choose it. We are all struggling to become perfect, so our job is to simply love one another."

It's common knowledge that the best way to teach anyone is through the power of example. If we live our lives as though someone is constantly looking over our shoulder (and in fact, Someone is!), the world around us will sit up and take notice. Cathy Barclay, my good friend who joined the Church about ten years ago, once wrote to me, "Always living what you believe, in a world as we do today, gives plenty of opportunity to speak of the truth. People are always interested in those who choose good."

Why is that? Why are people so curious about "those who choose good"? Believe it or not, even the reporters I dealt with during my Miss America year kept coming back to that. Even though my answers were considered "boring" and certainly not intriguing enough for tabloid journalism, they would still ask me about being such a "goody-goody." Why? My guess is that people everywhere struggle with day-to-day choices and wonder what it is that gives an individual the strength, even the courage, to "choose good" when it is not always the popular path.

It is difficult to predict how our behavior will affect another person—or how long it will take for that to happen. You might know someone for years and yet feel that you have had no influence on them. Other times, a brief chance meeting will have an enormous impact. In a different setting and over trivial matters, really, I remember being affected in such a way by a ten-year-old girl in a small Kansas town. She did not change my life, but she almost ruined my day with a comment she made. I'm sure she never guessed that she had the power to affect a grown-up that way with such a simple comment.

I was making an appearance in a Kansas grocery store, sitting at a table and signing autographs while a few patrons waited in line. I had been there a couple of hours when it was this little girl's turn for an autograph. She said, "Hi." Then after she had given me her name to write on the picture, she said to me, "You know, that dress looks awful on you." What do you say to a comment such as that? I thanked her for her observation, and she left with my autograph in her left hand and a little bit of my pride in her right.

For the rest of the day, I felt terrible because I had on an ugly dress, or so I had been told, and I didn't have a chance to change into something else. I couldn't quit thinking about what she had said. I kept trying to tell myself that she was only ten and that she hardly lived in the fashion capital of the world, so what would she know? But the truth is, her simple comment, regardless of her qualifications, had the power to stick with me and affect how I felt about myself.

That's the way it is with words: Once they leave our mouths, we cannot retract them or erase their effect. And we have no control over which person they will affect or how deeply. This is also true of our actions.

During the 1988 presidential campaign, one potential candidate seriously impaired his chances and consequently withdrew from the race when it was discovered that he was involved in an illicit affair. A few months later, the young woman with whom he had been involved was interviewed on television by Barbara Walters. Toward the end of the interview, Barbara asked the young woman this question: "What lessons have you learned and what advice would you give your younger sister?"

The politician's mistress replied quite sincerely and remorsefully, "I would say to her, think before you act. There is a consequence for every act." Then she paused for a moment before concluding: "And other people are affected by your actions."

She was right. In those few sentences she expressed a universal truth. Every human being is linked to society, and what we do and how we behave doesn't have an impact only on us. John Donne expressed it well: "No man is an island, entire of itself; every man is a piece of the continent, a part of the main; if a clod be washed away by the sea, Europe is the less, as well as if a promontory were, as well as if a manor of thy friends or of thine own were; any man's death diminishes me, because I am involved in mankind" (*Devotions* [written 1623], *Meditation XVII*).

As members of The Church of Jesus Christ of Latter-day Saints, we have twice the responsibility to mankind: We not only leave an impression of ourselves with each person we meet, but we also create an impression of the gospel of Jesus Christ. We incur an obligation when we are baptized and when we renew that baptismal covenant by partaking weekly of the sacrament. Our actions, our words, our very lives have an ines-timable power to create a lasting impression and to influence others. "Think before you act" (or *speak,* for that matter) is good advice. Your message, good or bad, is clear and often unforgettable.

The day after I won Miss America, I was approached by a gentleman who had seen my press conference the night before, as well as the headline that proclaimed, "Mormon Sunday School Teacher Wins Crown!" All he said to me was, "When I heard you were a Mormon, I knew you stood for everything right." Of course, I beamed and accepted the compliment. But in that same moment I was quickly made aware that *I* had not yet proven anything. The positive Mormon reputation had already been established for me by the other Latter-day Saints with whom this man had come in contact. He was assuming I would measure up, and what occurred to me was that it was not entirely the reputation of the Church that would be on trial, but in addition, my reputation as a member. My experi-ence has been that most of the people I have met are aware of the goodness I am *supposed* to represent. If I were to fail, it would, of course, reflect poorly on the Church, but it would be *my* reputation that would be most tarnished. "When I heard you were a Mormon, I knew you stood for everything right." That's a lot to live up to.

I once read a short article by JeaNette Goates Smith in the *New Era* that illustrates precisely what I hope to convey. The article, titled "The Shirt I Was Afraid to Wear," tells of a T-shirt that the author was afraid to wear because the letters "BYU" were written on it. JeaNette felt that if she wore the T-shirt in Florida, where she lived, and did anything rude or inappropriate—even something as small as cutting in front of another car—someone would surely identify her as a Mormon and think that's the way *all* members of the Church behaved. It could stop them, she worried, from even wanting to learn more about the Church. The shirt lay untouched at the bottom of her drawer until she realized that she could do some *good* while wearing the T-shirt, thus helping others form a favorable impression of Latter-day Saints. "Why not try it?" she asked herself.

One day she gained the courage to wear the BYU T-shirt to the mall. The moment she put the shirt on, she felt almost like a missionary for the Church! When she was purchasing a dress, the cashier noticed her T-shirt and asked her if she had gone to BYU. Before JeaNette could reply, the cashier told her that she, too, had attended BYU, but later she had married out of the Church and hadn't been to church since. The two exchanged telephone numbers, and JeaNette told the cashier the location and times of Sunday meetings. Before JeaNette left, the other woman had promised to see her at church the next Sunday. Thrilled to have discovered the blessings that come to missionaries, JeaNette changed her mind about the BYU shirt: "At home that afternoon, I washed my T-shirt, dried and folded it, and placed it in my drawer on top of the stack. I knew I would wear it again soon" (see JeaNette Goates Smith, "The Shirt I Was Afraid to Wear," *New Era,* February 1993, pp. 26–27).

No matter where we live or how ordinary we think our life is, we all run across people who can be influenced positively by our good example. It's true that we can't change the past—but the wonderful news is that we can change the future. Whether your example has been ideal or less than stellar, I suggest you start making a good impression today. Remind yourself what kind of reputation you want to create—and then start living in such a way as to make it happen!

CHAPTER 13

BUILDING UNSHAKABLE CONFIDENCE

Throughout this book, I have tried to be specific in discussing the areas in which we especially need to stand firm, the areas that tend to separate us most noticeably from our friends, associates, and neighbors who are not of our faith. I realize that as I continually emphasize "standing firm," there are probably many levels of confidence and courage among us as members of the Church. Each one of us, in fact, has higher levels of confidence in some areas and less confidence in regard to other issues. And for many whose beliefs are strong, perhaps courage is still weak. It helps to remember that even the great Apostle Peter had his moments of weakness. He denied his Master and his best friend three times in one night.

How do you build your confidence so it is unshakable? How do you lift your courage to face any fear undaunted? How do you remain calm in the face of intimidation? My first answer is a simple two-part formula: Pray always! Listen to the Spirit!

This true story shows how my dad put himself in what could be seen as considerable danger while following the promptings of the Holy Spirit. His actions were both inspired and courageous as he showed his unwavering faith in the Lord, his surest foundation.

While our family was living in Latin America, Dad often piloted his own single-engine airplane. Because of his good reputation as both a pilot and a member of the Church, he was once challenged in an unusual way.

At the time, he was serving as both a branch president and a district president. He was also very well known by many government and business leaders in the Latin American country where he lived and worked.

One day a minister from a Protestant church came to Dad with an unusual request. "Mr. Wells," the minister said, "You are a good Christian gentleman and a leader of your church, one who has served God in many ways. I have a major problem. I have prayed for guidance and have been led to you for help."

Intrigued, Dad said, "Thank you for the compliment, but what can I do to help?"

The minister replied, "I have just heard by radio from one of our mission outposts in the jungle that a woman there is extremely ill. The nursing station at the mission is inadequate, and after conferring with the doctors here, it has been determined the woman needs to be immediately evacuated and brought here to the hospital to be operated on, or she will surely die. Her life is in jeopardy. We need your help!"

Dad had often been called upon for charitable donations, and this seemed like a situation where he could easily help, so he responded readily, "I'll be glad to pay for the charter flight to bring her out. How much money do you need?"

The reverend quickly answered, "No, it's not money that we need, it is *you*. Have you read the paper this morning?"

My father replied that he had, but the only thing he had noted was the news of an invasion by some dissident rebels from across the border. Had he missed something?

"With the threat of the invasion, the government has grounded all civilian planes, and even a mercy flight to save a life cannot be authorized. I have come to you because I know you have influence in the right places. You are viewed as a priest in your church and a trusted friend of the government. I feel you can get permission to make the flight."

As recently as the night before, Dad had taught a family home evening lesson to his family on being prepared to serve others in a Christlike way. He had discussed the parable of the good Samaritan and read the Savior's own words about providing for the sick and the needy: "Inasmuch as ye have done it unto one of the least of these my brethren, ye have done it unto me" (Matthew 25:40).

Now he was being called upon to practice what he had preached. My father felt his priesthood and his religion were all of a sudden on the line. He knew he needed to respond by doing what he could to help save the woman's life. It is what the Savior would have done. The day's business was quickly set aside, and Dad telephoned one of his friends, the country's director of civil aviation.

"Señor Alvarado, this is your old friend and flying colleague, Bob Wells. How are you this morning?" he began.

The leader of the country's Civil Aviation Affairs responded warmly, and Dad continued, "My friend, I understand that all civil flights are grounded, but I need permission for one air taxi flight out to the Anglican mission in the jungle, about 120 miles from here. Or I need authorization to fly my plane out there. There is a woman there who must be brought in for an emergency operation. How about it? Can you arrange that for me, my friend?"

Señor Alvarado didn't immediately reply. Then, after a few moments of silence, he said, "Mr. Wells, it is very difficult for me to turn you down, but please understand, I am only a man under orders from the military. Because of the threat of invasion, all civilian planes have been grounded. Troops have orders to fire at any nonmilitary aircraft that even moves."

Further pleadings didn't do any good. Finally, Dad put down the phone and turned to the minister. "I don't know what to do. You heard the conversation—he says he can do nothing. He would be fired if he acted otherwise, and he says the troops are all around the airport with orders to shoot at any civilian or private plane that even moves."

The minister responded very softly, "I already knew all of that. I have spoken with the air taxi pilots. I am here because the Spirit tells me that you are the only one who can save this poor woman's life."

Dad said a silent prayer, then picked up the phone and dialed directly to another acquaintance, the military general in charge of the country's air force. The general had courted influence from the large bank Dad represented. Based on that relationship, it was worth a try.

After the usual telephone courtesies, Dad went right to the point and asked for a military plane to make the mercy flight, with himself as pilot or copilot, if needed.

The general was courteous but firm. "Roberto, I truly regret the situation, but I can neither allow you to make a flight with your plane nor with one of ours. The president of the country has personally ordered the grounding of all flights other than those necessary to defend against a possible invasion.

So you see, I can do nothing to help you." Other options were discussed, but no solution was reached.

Dad turned to the minister after hanging up. "You heard my end of the conversation again. I have done everything possible. In effect, he just told me to let her die."

The minister persisted. "All I know, Mr. Wells, is that I was led to you for help. There is still something you can do. I just feel it."

It is really unusual to have a minister from some other faith insist that the Spirit has prompted *him* to have a Mormon priesthood holder perform the minister's duty. But that was what happened. Praying silently again, Dad picked up the phone once more.

This time he worked his way up through the complicated bureaucracy of the nation's military dictatorship in an effort to reach the president of the country. The large and prestigious U.S. bank Dad worked for had been a welcome presence in that Latin American country. The president had met with Dad on numerous occasions to work out the details of opening the bank's offices and operations. Later, when the bank's presence had begun to benefit his country, the president had been very cordial and even deferential whenever he and Dad met.

Finally, Dad was able to get to the man who was closest to the president, his personal secretary, who seemed to be more powerful than even the cabinet members. The secretary understood the situation as explained but said that the president was in a closed session with his generals, which would last until the emergency was over. No calls would be taken. However, Dad was able to get the man to agree to try to get to the president with the request to authorize this one mercy flight.

After a few minutes' delay, the secretary returned to the phone and said, "Mr. Wells, I could not interrupt. I stood there and waited for an opening, but it was too tense. I am sorry, but I cannot help you further. The woman will just have to die."

Helpless, Dad put down the phone and turned to the minister. "I can't get through to him. I don't have any other options."

Unwilling to give up, however, Dad thought of one other thing. The main airport with the paved runway had been closed, and the troops there were ready to shoot down any plane that might attempt to fly. And Dad knew the threat was real. During a previous attempted coup, a civilian plane had flown overhead, dropping leaflets intended to stir up the population against the military government and giving instructions on how to organize an insurrection. Dad realized that the government, in an effort to prevent any similar incidents, would shoot down any plane trying to fly out of the big airport. But maybe, he reasoned, the air club on the opposite side of the city, with only a grass runway, had been forgotten.

With that in mind, he thought of a risky plan. He said to the minister, "Let's drive to the air club to see if the troops have closed down operations there."

As they approached the air club hangars, Dad explained his plan to the minister: "I have been praying for a solution, and maybe this will work. If there are no troops, we will just take the club's green Stinson and make the flight. I have permission to use the plane because I loaned the money to the air club to buy it. Club rules require that it be fully gassed up after every flight, and it is tied down off to the side of the main hangar.

There is no key required. It is ready to fly the moment the master switch is turned on."

The minister responded, "But what if there are troops guarding the air club?" Dad had no answer and could only shake his head.

Arriving at the air club, they saw about ten soldiers, armed with rifles, standing around in front of the hangars. Dad recognized the officer in charge as one of the air force captains with whom he had flown as copilot. Dad prayed silently to know what to do, and a plan developed when he saw that the green, somewhat antique Stinson airplane was not tied down and was sitting unguarded to one side of where the officer and troops were standing.

He whispered to the minister, "You walk to the far side of the plane, open the door, and get in—don't say a word."

Together they walked quickly to the plane. Each opened his unlocked door, swung up into the cabin of the aircraft, and slammed his door. Dad immediately found the master switch, flipped it on, hit the primer twice, turned the magneto switches to "both," and hit the starter. Miraculously, the engine caught on the first try and roared to life.

The officer and the troops immediately came running toward the stationary plane. Gesturing for Dad to cut the engine, the officer shouted something Dad couldn't hear. Dad slid open the pilot's side window, so the officer could see him clearly, but kept the engine running. The officer gave another signal to cut the engine by drawing his finger quickly across his throat. In reply, Dad waggled his finger in sign language to say, "No, I will not cut the engine." The officer then unsnapped the flap on his holster and took out his automatic pistol. The threat was very real.

Following a prompting, Dad stuck his left arm out of the window and, making a toy pistol of his hand, pointed his index finger as if it were a gun barrel at the plane's engine and wiggled his thumb like the hammer of a pistol. With his right hand he moved his index finger back and forth to say in sign language, "Don't shoot me—shoot the engine!"

Advancing the throttle slightly, Dad continued to look the officer steadily in the eye and released the brakes. The plane rolled forward slowly over the grass. My father waited until he was well past the officer, who was staring at him with a quizzical look on his face, then accelerated. Without regard to the wind sock or the usual path across the field for taking off, Dad just increased his speed until the plane lifted off. Flying at a low altitude and away from known military bases, Dad found the large river and followed it north. He flew over the jungle along the river's banks to be better camouflaged from above, in the event that fighter planes were sent after them. He hoped the faded green color of the plane would make it difficult to spot them against the green jungle below.

They landed at the mission, picked up the critically ill passenger, and flew back over the same route. Before he took off for the return trip, Dad had the mission radio the hospital to have an ambulance meet them at the grass airstrip.

They could see the ambulance waiting as they landed and observed that the soldiers, who should have been shooting at them, were keeping a respectful distance. He noted also that the officer who had been in charge had been replaced by another officer whom Dad didn't know.

The plane landed safely. The woman was operated on and her life was saved. Through the president's secretary, Dad made an apology to the president of the country, explaining that he had been compelled to act in good conscience and for a humanitarian need. Dad later learned that the officer who had not followed orders was disciplined and put under house arrest for a time. But the matter was never pursued. Dad assumed the government did not want to cause an international incident or risk offending the U.S. bank, which was providing an economic benefit to the country. The next time Dad saw the nation's president, he apologized. The president simply said, "I'm glad it turned out well for all concerned."

A few weeks after the mercy flight, my father ran into the captain who had been disciplined. Apologizing for ignoring his warnings, Dad asked the captain why he had not put a .45 caliber bullet into the plane's engine. The officer smiled wanly and answered, "Señor Wells, I am a man used to obeying orders, no matter the consequences. I would not have hesitated to shoot you, but when you signaled to shoot the engine instead, I had a thought come into my mind that I still marvel at. I thought, 'As a pilot, I just cannot ruin a perfectly good airplane engine.'"

Acting under the influence of the Spirit, Dad was able to know what to do. When he tells this story, he testifies that the Lord guided him and softened the heart of the officer so that he and his minister friend could accomplish their mission.

I have heard this story often throughout my life, and it has become one of my favorites of all the adventures Dad has experienced. Every time I hear it, I find myself awed by not only how brave and bold Dad was in the face of real consequences but how receptive he was to the promptings the Lord gave him. His trust in the Lord saved his life and others.

We each face difficult circumstances—perhaps not as dangerous as this one, but nevertheless nerve-wracking or even terrifying—times when we need to act boldly, plant our feet, and become immovable in our resolve. By trusting in the Lord, we will be prepared.

Again, to build unshakable confidence we follow a two-part formula of first praying and then listening for answers. My second answer to the question of how to build that kind of confidence is much more comprehensive, taking into account a number of factors in our preparation for confronting our own fear along with the questions others may throw at us. I discovered this (though it's certainly no secret!), the best answer I've heard, in my own home ward in Gospel Doctrine class. Brother Steve Bateman is the well-prepared teacher who kindly allowed me to borrow his research and the information he shared on the topic in class one Sunday.

The scriptural base for building unshakable confidence is this scripture from the Doctrine and Covenants section 27:

> Take upon you my whole armor, that ye may be able to withstand the evil day, having done all, that ye may be able to stand.
>
> Stand, therefore, having your loins girt about with truth, having on the breastplate of righteousness, and your feet shod with the preparation of the gospel of peace, which I have sent mine angels to commit unto you;
>
> Taking the shield of faith wherewith ye shall be able to quench all the fiery darts of the wicked;
>
> And take the helmet of salvation, and the sword of my Spirit, which I will pour out upon you, and my word which

I shall reveal unto you, and be agreed as touching all things whatsoever ye ask of me, and be faithful until I come, and ye shall be caught up, that where I am ye shall be also. Amen. (Verses 15–18)

Brother Bateman read to the class an excerpt from *Studies in Scripture:* "We may all stand faithfully and overcome the things of this world, and be saved at the Lord's coming and partake of the Sacrament with him, if we will put on God's whole armor, and keep it on. No one can escape the battle; Satan makes war upon each servant of the Lord. To stand successfully and come off conqueror, we must wear the armor of the Lord" (Leon R. Hartshorn, "Where I Am Ye Shall Be Also," in *Studies in Scripture,* 8 vols., ed. Robert L. Millet and Kent P. Jackson [Salt Lake City: Deseret Book Company, 1989], 1:128–29).

I have often read about and been taught the importance of putting on the "armor of God," but this time, the *necessity* of being well protected struck me with particular emphasis. No soldier goes into battle unprotected, and as the hymn says, "We are all enlisted" (*Hymns,* no. 250). Though I had never thought of my conversations with friends or strangers as any kind of battle when discussing things of a spiritual nature, it could still be considered a battlefield, where there are those waiting to capture the wounded. In fact, we are cautioned never to enter into any kind of arguments or "Bible bashing" with those we are trying to teach, because if we do, the Spirit will leave us.

The adversary does his most effective work in covert, not overt, ways. He uses subtle means to keep the honest in heart from finding answers to their questions about the real meaning of life. Thus we need the full armor of God, in place at all times, or the effectiveness of that armor is compromised.

What are the parts of armor we should put on? How are they indispensable to me in my everyday conversations and encounters? Let's create a mental picture of what a full suit of armor might look like.

First, the wearer of armor has "loins girt about with truth." Brother Hartshorn comments, "The girdle of armor that goes about the loins [is] the armor of truth. . . . A servant of the Lord wears the spiritual armor of 'truth' to protect his virtue. Elder Harold B. Lee wrote: 'Truth is to be the substance of which the girdle about your loins is to be formed if your virtue and vital strength is to be safeguarded'" (ibid., p. 129).

Second, we arm ourselves with the "breastplate of righteousness." Some gospel scholars feel the breastplate is a symbol of the protection of the heart. *Studies in Scripture* explains the phrase thus: "One of the beatitudes says: 'Blessed are the pure in heart: for they shall see God' (Matt. 5:8). . . . To be pure in heart we must keep impurities out. . . . Righteousness means meeting the standards of that which is morally right and just" (ibid., p. 129).

Third, we must have "feet . . . shod . . . with the preparation of the gospel of peace." Elder Harold B. Lee wrote, "Your feet, which are to represent your goals or objectives in life, are to be shod. Shod with what? 'With the preparation of the gospel of peace.' . . . [The Apostle Paul] knew that preparedness is the way to victory and that 'eternal vigilance is the price of safety.' Fear is the penalty of unpreparedness and aimless dawdling with opportunity" (*Stand Ye in Holy Places* [Salt Lake City: Deseret Book Company, 1974], p. 333).

Next, we are protected by the "shield of faith." "When persecution, heartbreak, temptation, disappointment, illness, etc., come into the life of a Latter-day Saint, the first thing he should do is get behind the shield of faith. He must let the Lord help him; if he does not, then Satan's fiery darts may wound him spiritually. Some have sustained so many wounds that their recovery is lengthy, and there are some who have never recovered" (Leon R. Hartshorn, *Studies in Scripture,* 1:129).

Now for the "helmet of salvation." This part of the armor "protect[s] our mind, our ability to think properly. . . . Wilford Woodruff said that Oliver Cowdery at one time had a powerful testimony, but he 'yielded to the temptation of the evil one.' Oliver began to think that he was smarter than Joseph Smith and wanted to direct the Prophet; thus Oliver apostatized. . . . His thinking deviated from the truth first, and soon his actions followed" (ibid.).

And now for the final piece of armor—the "sword of the Spirit." This is the word of God. "The Lord never intended that his servants, his soldiers, fight only a defensive battle. He desires that we be on the offensive and help overcome evil, free mankind from the terrible effects of evil, and prepare the earth for the return of the Savior. The sword is primarily an offensive weapon. We are to take the sword of the Spirit, the word of God. Thus we are to study the scriptures, listen to the voices of the living prophets, and have the companionship of the Holy Ghost as we move forward in God's service" (ibid., p. 130).

In conclusion, "one who wears God's whole armor is happy and confident in the battle against evil. One who does not is devastated by the struggle. We must wear the armor always throughout life, keep it polished through service, and keep it in good repair through repentance" (ibid.).

For as long as I can remember, my best and most immediate examples of how to effectively wear the armor of God at all times are my own parents. In my mind, I think of missionary work as being on the "front lines," and all my life my mom and dad have been anxiously engaged, right in the thick of things. And there is nowhere else they would rather be; they see missionary work as an adventure.

I have seen them live in truth and righteousness, fully prepared in their studies of the gospel. Their faith has shielded them in times of disappointment and tragedy. Their thoughts do not betray them, but rather spur them on to righteous action. And I witnessed them raise the "sword of the Spirit" by being bold in proclaiming the gospel and in preparing men and women everywhere for the Savior's return.

How grateful I am to have a clear picture of what true soldiers of Christ look like!

CHAPTER 14

REAL SUCCESS IN THE "REAL" WORLD

W hen we speak of the "real" world, what do we
mean? Sometimes we think of the real world as a
sort of "school of hard knocks," where nothing is
simply handed to us and where we learn things the hard way.
We also refer to the real world as the place where the majority
of the population embraces, or at least accepts, immorality,
worldliness, and other forms of unrighteousness. Would it follow, then, that a life lived strictly in accordance with God's
teachings is a life of fantasy? Maybe so. But I would rather live
in a fantasy world—inside a personal cocoon, if you will—surrounded by gospel principles and righteous standards than I
would in an environment where immorality, dishonesty, and
selfishness are the norm.

During my year as Miss America, I recall well one particular visit to Houston. The members of the Church there saw to
it that I was not bored for a minute! I was asked if I would be
interested in a visit to NASA with LDS astronaut Don Lind as
my personal guide. Naturally, I was thrilled! It was such an
honor to spend the morning with Brother Lind, and I was fas-
cinated by all he had to show me. I even got to sit in the shuttle
simulator. As we looked around the interior, he described the
seated position of the astronauts as they leave the earth's atmosphere—a position that, to the rest of us, looked upside down!

I asked him how it felt to fly upside down. He replied, "Oh, I never felt upside down. I might have seen the earth above me through the window, but I was always right side up!" It occurred to me that in many ways, we as members of the Church might be made to feel *we* are the ones who are "upside down" when, in fact, it is the rest of the world hanging upside down while we try to remain true and "right side up" to the Lord's commandments.

In a magazine devoted to "the world of science," I read a fascinating article, titled "In the Earth but Not of It." The article reported that "the earth's inner core might as well be another planet. This 1,500-mile-wide sphere, made not of rock but of solid iron, is divided from the rest of the planet by the outer core—a moat of churning liquid iron, 1,300 miles thick. In 1996 it was reported that this planet within a planet even spins at its own rate, outpacing the rest of Earth by about a quarter turn per century." The article explains that the liquid iron in the "moat" is so hot that it's as thin as water, "so the inner core should be free to spin on its own, like a beach ball in a bathtub" (*Discover*, January 1997, p. 19).

Hmm. Another planet. How many times has someone said *you* are from another planet? Sometimes that's the way we feel—either upside down compared to the rest of the world or from another planet. A description of the earth's inner core could describe members of The Church of Jesus Christ of Latter-day Saints as well. I think we would all love to be compared to "solid iron," different from the ordinary rock of the rest of the world. To be solid iron is to be impenetrable by the whims of the world.

The solid iron core of earth is "divided from the rest of the planet" by a "moat of churning liquid iron." I will call that moat the gospel of Jesus Christ. Now for the best part of the comparison: "This planet within a planet even spins at its own rate, *outpacing the rest of Earth.*"

Yes, by living our standards we may occasionally feel "out of step" with the rest of our community, even with society in general. But if we are solid in our resolve to maintain our own pace, our allowing the gospel to set the pace in our lives will ultimately help us to outpace the rest of the world. As Paul said, "Be not conformed to this world: but be ye transformed by the renewing of your mind, that ye may prove what is that good, and acceptable, and perfect, will of God" (Romans 12:2).

In the world, success is often measured by how famous or how wealthy one is. I used to accept that definition of success, until I experienced a taste of it. For one year, as a twenty-year-old, I was treated like a movie star. As Miss America, I was granted instant celebrity status. People who may not have even known my name lined up to obtain my autograph or to have their picture taken with me. I was presented with flowers at every stop, provided with limousine service, given gifts, and presented with a number of "keys to the city." The press was everywhere, and they asked me about everything. After a month of that kind of treatment, I recall thinking, *Is this what some people struggle all their lives for? To be famous?* My guess is that those who yearn for fame and then achieve it end up reacting to it much the same way I did. It was not very fulfilling and sometimes a pain. Being famous is not a ticket to happiness or a sure source of joy.

I discovered that being famous (for all of one year!) made it difficult to just "hang out" with friends or family members in a public place. And since those relationships are prime to me, I resented the fact that I was so often noticed and that I was rarely able to follow my own schedule or do my own thing. Because of the volume of demands and interruptions, life was hectic and not always enjoyable. I very quickly discovered that I am not a person who needs or even likes the spotlight, though with experience I have learned how to be comfortable there. Ironically, even though I had very much wanted to be noticed and liked all during my elementary, junior high, and high school years, after a month of constantly being looked at because I was now "famous," I was ready to go back to being anonymous. Believe it or not, I actually *wanted* to be a wallflower.

Why? The things that had always made me the happiest—my family, my understanding of my divine heritage as a daughter of God, and my testimony of Jesus Christ and his gospel—were not to be found in the spotlight of public attention. Oh, I got to do some exciting things, to be sure. It was heady to visit President Ronald Reagan in the White House and to play golf with Bob Hope, but none of these things contributed anything lasting to my overall happiness and contentment. What I discovered was that "fame and fortune" in and of themselves don't provide a sense of fulfillment or joy. The truth of that is easily seen in the ruined lives of many rich and famous people who, in spite of their wealth and fame, are seemingly never satisfied. It is one thing to work to reach a level of financial independence that will provide safety and comfort for your family, but quite another to sacrifice family and values in an empty search for a jazzier sports car, more extravagant vacations, or flashier clothing and accessories. I know many people who have made such an exchange, and not one of them is genuinely happy, despite what they may have accumulated in the way of worldly treasures.

That is not to say that people who put their families first and who strive to live by the Spirit can't succeed in a financial sense. I know a number of people who have exemplary family lives—who read the scriptures, have family prayer, serve in the Church, frequently attend the temple, and contribute significantly of their time and money to worthy causes—and who are still able to afford the "good life." But that is often the exception rather than the rule. Wealth can serve as a distraction that leads people away from spiritual pursuits and good works. That is why we are so often warned by the leaders of the Church to beware of the love of riches. It's not the coins and the bills that do the damage—they are simply inanimate objects. It is the obsessive behavior that coins and bills often attract that we must beware of. Those who are blessed with a surplus are in a position to do a great deal of good, if their vision does not become distorted so that they lose perception.

We often hear of those who relentlessly pursue that which is difficult to get. Just this past Christmas, I was amused by the mania that one twenty-eight-dollar toy created. Parents all over the country were desperate to get their hands on this toy. Soon "scalpers" saw their opportunity and began selling these toys on the street corners and through newspaper ads for tremendously inflated prices. As much as a thousand dollars was paid for this twenty-eight-dollar toy! Now, if there were a tag attached to a young son or daughter or to a wife or a husband that simply said, "This item cannot be purchased—it is priceless," well, it seems to me that a lot more people would pursue those things, latch onto them, and never let go.

Some people figure that out when they are young. Others seem to make a lifetime of mistakes before they ultimately reach an understanding of what is really important in life. But in the end, *everyone* will understand. Someone once said that no one ever lay on their deathbed wishing they had worked more or played more golf. Everyone who comes to that point wishes they had given more of themselves to the important people in their lives.

There is an account in the New Testament of a rich young man who approached Christ, perhaps even knelt at his feet, asking, "Good Master, what good thing shall I do, that I may have eternal life?"

Jesus replied, "If thou wilt enter into life, keep the commandments."

The young man, who was apparently honest and sincere, responded, "All these things have I kept from my youth up: what lack I yet?"

Jesus said, "If thou wilt be perfect, go and sell that thou hast, and give to the poor, and thou shalt have treasure in heaven: and come and follow me."

The young man had apparently attached himself so tightly to his wealth that he could not bear such a wrenching separation. His wealth blinded him to what was of real value and worth. He was unable to relinquish it, and "he went away sorrowful" (see Matthew 19:16–22).

Another lesson the Master taught on this topic was through the parable of the rich man and Lazarus, found in Luke 16:19–25:

> There was a certain rich man, which was clothed in purple and fine linen, and fared sumptuously every day:

And there was a certain beggar named Lazarus, which was laid at his gate, full of sores,

And desiring to be fed with the crumbs which fell from the rich man's table: moreover the dogs came and licked his sores.

And it came to pass, that the beggar died, and was carried by the angels into Abraham's bosom: the rich man also died, and was buried;

And in hell he lift up his eyes, being in torments, and seeth Abraham afar off, and Lazarus in his bosom.

And he cried and said, Father Abraham, have mercy on me, and send Lazarus, that he may dip the tip of his finger in water, and cool my tongue; for I am tormented in this flame.

But Abraham said, Son, remember that thou in thy lifetime receivedst thy good things, and likewise Lazarus evil things: but now he is comforted, and thou are tormented.

Commenting on this parable, James E. Talmage wrote:

The rich man's fate was not the effect of riches, nor was the rest into which Lazarus entered the resultant of poverty. Failure to use his wealth aright, and selfish satisfaction with the sensuous enjoyment of earthly things to the exclusion of all concern for the needs or privations of his fellows, brought the one under condemnation; while patience in suffering, faith in God and such righteous life as is implied though not expressed, insured happiness to the other. The proud self-sufficiency of the rich man, who lacked nothing that wealth could furnish and who kept aloof from the needy and suffering, was his besetting sin. (*Jesus the Christ,* 19th ed. [Salt Lake City: The Church of Jesus Christ of Latter-day Saints, 1949], pp. 468–69)

I recently watched an interview with singer Barbra Streisand conducted by Barbara Walters. Obviously, Barbra has been "rich and famous" for quite some time, and as the two women talked together, Ms. Walters asked Barbra about the recent sale of her beautiful Malibu mansion and the decision the popular singer made to put absolutely everything in it up for auction.

"You have spent a lifetime collecting these beautiful pieces of furniture and works of art—why sell it all?"

To which Ms. Streisand replied, "I want to simplify my life."

That is good advice. We would all do well to evaluate the "junk" or excess baggage in our lives—both tangible and intangible—and then get rid of it. Simplify your life.

Before you launch out into the world, it would be a useful exercise to make a list of your dreams and goals—the things you want to achieve and become. It would also be revealing to write down, next to each item, the *reason* you are pursuing these things. *Why* do you want to be recognized by your peers and the world? *Why* do you want to become a millionaire or whatever else you're pursuing? What is the driving force behind your ambitions? There are *dreams,* and then there are *priorities.* Sometimes the two are compatible, but what if they aren't?

If you are at the stage where you are poised to leap from college into the "real world," creating such a list can be a valuable measuring stick, and a reality check, as you forge ahead in your career and life pursuits. It might be interesting, in the first week after your first child is born, to take out your list and evaluate it. Your *whys* will probably change and become a little more meaningful. If you've got any competitive juices, you probably want to be at the top. No matter what the discipline, being on top feels good. For a while. And then what? What is actually *at* the top?

One of my favorite books is *Hope for the Flowers* by Trina

Paulus, in which the author tells the story of Stripe, a hungry young caterpillar.

Stripe joins a large number of squirming, pushing caterpillars, each of which is struggling to climb a great column that rises into the air and disappears into the clouds. Stripe sees that the caterpillars are all intent on trying to reach the top of the column, but since its top is obscured by the clouds, he has no idea what he might find there. Even so, Stripe pushes upward with his fellows.

The journey is not easy. Stripe is pushed and kicked and stepped on from every direction. Climb, or be stepped on, seems to be everyone's motto.

Full of agitation, Stripe asks a fellow crawler, "Do you know what's happening?"

" 'I just arrived myself,' said the other. 'Nobody has time to explain; they're so busy trying to get wherever they're going up there.'

" 'But what's at the top?' continued Stripe.

" 'No one knows that either, but it must be awfully good because everybody's rushing there. Goodbye; I've got no more time!' "

The story goes on at some length. The thing Stripe learns is that his mindless struggle to climb over others and get to the top is a futile, pointless endeavor. His ambition costs him for a time the things that would be of true worth to him—companionship and love—and it is not until he gives up his empty quest that he reaches his full potential and becomes a beautiful butterfly (see Trina Paulus, *Hope for the Flowers* [New York: Paulist Press, 1972]).

Whenever I have competed for a job, an honor, or a

position, I have tried to enter the arena with two objectives: first, to do my best (to outperform *myself),* and second, to simply have fun. As for those against whom I was competing, I only wanted to befriend them. That way, whether or not I won, it was enjoyable to applaud the people I had come to like. By the same token, should *I* win, it would make it easier for my fellow competitors to support me. I haven't always been able to make friends with everyone, but I hope it is not because I did not try.

Theoretically, success should equal happiness. But very often, by putting success first, we forfeit happiness. It doesn't need to be that way.

My husband and I have a very good friend, Bruce Brainard, a successful artist who has adopted for his life's philosophy the Lord's declaration "Seek not for riches but for wisdom, and behold, the mysteries of God shall be unfolded unto you, and then shall you be made rich. Behold, he that hath eternal life is rich" (D&C 6:7).

When Bruce decided to make art his profession, there were those who questioned his decision. He was cautioned that it would be difficult to earn a good living as a full-time artist. Bruce creates peaceful yet stunning landscapes filled with spiritual symbolism. He incorporates into his paintings subtle details that appeal on a subconscious level to the viewer's spirit. Some of Bruce's professors warned that his creations were too religious to have widespread appeal. His critics claimed they were made uncomfortable by Bruce's constant religious expressions, both on canvas and in his verbal descriptions of his work.

Bruce's response to criticism is this: "I have always tried to be about more noble pursuits, and in my artwork I always try to portray truth and beauty, hope and goodness. I delve in truth, not just in landscape, and I try to do it beautifully. Whether it sells or not is of no concern. Beauty is eternal, beauty is something that existed previously and will always exist. People are searching for beautiful things, and there will always be people who will buy such things. They might not be in the majority, but success in terms of dollars is not something I went out searching for. I just go and do my best."

About six months after he completed his undergraduate work, the quality of Bruce's work was recognized by a prominent art gallery with locations in Houston, Atlanta, Memphis, and New Orleans. They offered Bruce a contract to display and market his paintings, and he is now reaping the financial success he did not allow to motivate him. The demand for his serene and profound paintings continues to rise as he continues to adhere to his beliefs—and, in fact, galleries actually promote his spiritual themes since that is what their clients yearn for. One brochure said this: "Brainard's paintings have been characteristically viewed as metaphorically examining the nature of our existence. The calm, veiled sunsets or backlit fallen trees in his paintings evoke the longing for and separation from peacefulness and fulfillment. Light, as a symbol in these new paintings describes not a yearning, but an attainable invitation. Brainard's paintings describe a new beginning, a morning." Bruce chose truth as the measure of *real* success, and now he can barely keep up with the demand for his work. People are drawn to truth.

I like thoughts expressed in the poem "What Is *Real* Success?" by Tim Connor:

Everyone wants success, and yet they often don't
know when they have it.

For most, it is the maddening chase toward a better way of life or more of something. More fame, power, recognition, money, or

material stuff.

For some, it is the understanding of a loving partner, the love of their child, or the people that they can count on when life throws them a curve.

I am coming to believe that success is not more material wealth, but peace, happiness, contentment, and love.

Most of all love.

Real success is not to be sought after in the outer world, but discovered in your inner world. I am not condemning the stuff of life. We all want the things that life offers.

But we don't need as much

as we think we do.

Sooner or later you will discover that real success is to be found in loving relationships. With your family, friends, strangers, and anyone who crosses your path. It is kindness shared, support given and received, listening, giving, and caring.

These will endure while your car rusts, your toys break, and you tire of the temporary gratifications that bring you what you think is real.

What matters is people. What lasts is love. What counts are true friends, and if you treasure these you can count yourself a success.

(In *Be Proud of All You've Achieved: Poems on the Meaning of Success* [Boulder, Colo.: Blue Mountain Press], 1994)

Success isn't a place to be reached, as in "I made it to the top!" Success results from a series of choices. Who are your friends? What importance do you place on your family? How do you react to failures and unpredictable circumstances? Incidentally, one "secret of success" that I have learned along the way, ironically, has to do with failures. Everyone experiences failures. What counts is how we *react* to failure. If we learn to go on, we are headed toward success. To me, success is measured by who you are and what you stand for, not by what you've done.

Success is also loving and being loved. The day after the birth of our first daughter, Monica, I lay in bed, holding this tiny baby as she slept. My mom called to see how I was feeling. I don't remember feeling any pain, just pure contentment. I felt the fuzzy little head nestled close to my neck, and all I could say was, "Mom, there is absolutely nothing better in the whole world!" She chuckled knowingly.

Five years later, I was sitting with my feet propped up in our family room watching general conference on television. It was a beautiful, lazy Sunday afternoon. Monica came over to me, and for the first time (it seemed) since she had begun walking years ago, just wanted to sit on my lap and quietly let me hold her. She promptly fell asleep, and for the next hour, I couldn't think of anywhere else I would rather be. I remembered those words I had said to my mother, and two additional daughters later, I thought, *More than ever, it is so true!*

I have a list of highlights of my life. Some people might be surprised at the order in which I have them arranged. I would have to say that my being born is at the top (since it made everything else possible for me!), followed closely by my marriage in the Salt Lake Temple to the love of my life, my best friend and trusted adviser, Bob. Then there are the births of Monica, Nicole, and Sarah—arranged here chronologically and not in order of importance. Next comes receiving my degree from BYU, then my first contract with ESPN. Okay, maybe being Miss America takes the lead there. As I look back on that time, the whole year seemed almost unreal in my unbalanced twenty-year-old perception of its importance. It seemed nothing could ever top that worldly honor, and everything else seemed so mundane, even *ordinary* by comparison.

But with the passage of a few years, the events of my life have slipped into a different order of importance. I suppose that is what the passing of years brings—a sorting of the experiences that brought us pain or joy and a shifting of our priorities. All these things ought to result in the acquisition of some wisdom and maturity that ultimately helps us to "get real." We discover that real success—real joy—is to be found in the seemingly mundane things of life: a big squeeze from a child, an extraordinary sunset, a deep breath of fresh mountain air, the enjoyment of an oven-fresh, gooey chocolate chip cookie, or receiving a thank-you note from a grateful friend or neighbor. The happiness that many believe can be found in the glamour of the "real world" is not only temporary but, in all honesty, I believe it is a complete illusion. I wouldn't trade changing diapers and chauffeuring kids for anything, certainly not the life of a Miss America!

About six weeks after Monica was born, I wrote her a song, thinking as well of the vital role my own mom has played in my existence.

When you smile, the world smiles too.
When you laugh, I'll laugh with you.
When you love, it will come back to you,
That's what Mother says.

When you dream, they sometimes come true;
When you hope, things don't look so blue.
And when you're loved, your heart feels brand new,
That's what Mother says.

She says
It goes round and round
Till everyone finally hears
How simple is the sound
Of the happiness
We hold so dear.

When you're kind, folks are kind to you.
When you try, there's a lot that you can do,
And when you share, you'll find plenty for you,
That's what Mother says.

When you believe, then faith will comfort you.
When you seek, the answers will find you,
And when you pray, God will always hear you,
That's what Mother says . . .

She says
It goes round and round
Till everyone finally hears
How simple is the sound
Of the happiness
We hold so dear.

Success is simple. It begins—and ends—on the inside. There are a great many things in life that we cannot control, but we can determine how successful we *feel* by choosing what kind of success we are after. Achieving inner peace and being at peace with the world *is* success.

We *can* live in the world, walk side by side with the rest of the world in a search for better ways to exist and coexist, but yet we can keep our minds, our hearts, and our spirits consistently focused on ultimate success and acceptance in a very different world . . . a celestial one.

INDEX